"David Gibson has given the church a guide to the book of James and the issues it raises that is biblical, pastoral, accessible, reliable, wise, and patient. While focusing on James, Gibson helpfully explores its great topics by drawing on all of Scripture, wise reading, and pastoral experience to lead the reader into the gospel-based wholeness that the Lord desires to form in his people."

Dan Doriani, Professor of Biblical and Systematic Theology, Covenant Theological Seminary; Founder, Center for Faith and Work St. Louis

"No one ever says, 'When I grow up I want to be a hypocrite.' Yet most of us would have to admit that there are areas in our lives that simply don't line up with what we say we believe. In *Radically Whole*, David Gibson ably applies the straight-talk wisdom of the book of James to the areas of our lives that need to become conformed to the gospel we believe and the Savior we love."

Nancy Guthrie, Bible teacher; author

"If Martin Luther had been granted a future look at the pages of David Gibson's *Radically Whole* so that he could glimpse the overarching theme of the book of James and its symmetries (its 'melodic line'), he would not have voiced his infamous conclusion that it was 'a right strawy epistle' but would have recognized James as a profoundly substantial letter consonant with the gospel of grace. Gibson's penetrating exposition reveals that the grand unifying theme and purpose of James's letter is the perfection—the singular wholeness—of God's people. The book's nine chapters are laced with gripping theological insights and life-giving applications that lead toward biblical wholeness. Gibson is a devoted, hands-on pastor, so *Radically Whole* sparkles with memorable analogies and aphorisms that help the reader understand and put to work its truths. And, in doing this, it focuses us on Jesus, the only man in history who not only knew God's word but did it. This is a marvelous book, one that will be read, reread, underlined, and taken to heart—with enduring benefits."

R. Kent Hughes, Senior Pastor Emeritus, College Church Wheaton, Illinois

T0366387

"This excellent book gets right to the heart of James's message and his method. It is beautifully written, and David's exegetical skill and pastoral wisdom make it not only a compelling exposition of the letter but also a searching examination of the heart. I recommend it thoroughly for anyone who wants to understand James better, and to benefit spiritually in the process."

Andy Gemmill, Director of the Pastors' Training Course, Cornhill, Scotland

"The purpose of your consultation at the James clinic is to help you toward full spiritual health. You already know that you will first meet a different physician, a Dr. Gibson, who has studied under Dr. James for many years. He is a somewhat younger man, but his familiarity with Dr. James's inspired insights is impressive, as is the way he seems able to express the spirit and atmosphere of his teaching, as well as the central truth that Jesus Christ makes you whole. It is an idea that will recur in different ways as Dr. Gibson leads you, gently but firmly, through a comprehensive assessment process. And it begins with the first pages of *Radically Whole.* In its series of enriching consultations, David Gibson surefootedly provides the diagnosis, prescriptions, and prognosis we all need if we are to be made whole in Jesus Christ."

Sinclair B. Ferguson, Chancellor's Professor of Systematic Theology, Reformed Theological Seminary; Teaching Fellow, Ligonier Ministries

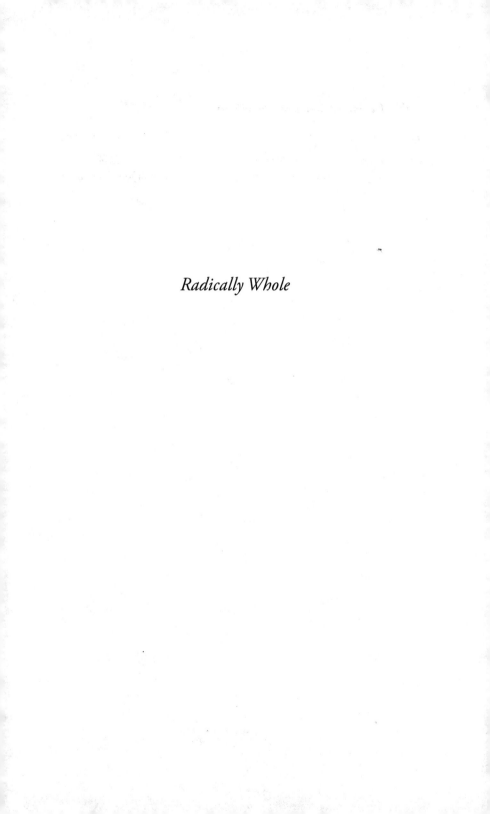

Radically Whole

Other Crossway Books by David Gibson

Living Life Backward: How Ecclesiastes Teaches Us to Live in Light of the End

From Heaven He Came and Sought Her: Definite Atonement in Historical, Biblical, Theological, and Pastoral Perspective, edited with Jonathan Gibson

Radically Whole

Gospel Healing for the Divided Heart

David Gibson

WHEATON, ILLINOIS

Radically Whole: Gospel Healing for the Divided Heart
Copyright © 2022 by David Gibson
Published by Crossway
　　　　1300 Crescent Street
　　　　Wheaton, Illinois 60187
Originally published by Inter-Varsity Press, 36 Causton Street, London, SW1P 4ST, England. Copyright © 2022 by David Gibson. North American edition published by permission of Inter-Varsity.
All rights reserved. No part of this publication may be reproduced, stored in a retrieval system, or transmitted in any form by any means, electronic, mechanical, photocopy, recording, or otherwise, without the prior permission of the publisher, except as provided for by USA copyright law. Crossway® is a registered trademark in the United States of America.
Cover design: Jordan Singer
Cover image: iStock
First printing 2022
Printed in the United States of America
Unless otherwise indicated, Scripture quotations are from the ESV® Bible (The Holy Bible, English Standard Version®), copyright © 2001 by Crossway, a publishing ministry of Good News Publishers. Used by permission. All rights reserved. The ESV text may not be quoted in any publication made available to the public by a Creative Commons license. The ESV may not be translated into any other language.
Scripture quotation marked NIV is taken from the Holy Bible, New International Version®, NIV®. Copyright © 1973, 1978, 1984, 2011 by Biblica, Inc.™ Used by permission of Zondervan. All rights reserved worldwide. www.zondervan.com. The "NIV" and "New International Version" are trademarks registered in the United States Patent and Trademark Office by Biblica, Inc.™
All emphases in Scripture quotations have been added by the author.
Trade paperback ISBN: 978-1-4335-8206-6
ePub ISBN: 978-1-4335-8209-7
PDF ISBN: 978-1-4335-8207-3
Mobipocket ISBN: 978-1-4335-8208-0

Library of Congress Cataloging-in-Publication Data
Names: Gibson, David, 1975– author.
Title: Radically whole : gospel healing for the divided heart / David Gibson.
Description: Wheaton, Illinois : Crossway, 2022. | Includes bibliographical references and index.
Identifiers: LCCN 2022011826 (print) | LCCN 2022011827 (ebook) | ISBN 9781433582066 (trade paperback) | ISBN 9781433582073 (pdf) | ISBN 9781433582080 (mobipocket) | ISBN 9781433582097 (epub)
Subjects: LCSH: Bible. James—Criticism, interpretation, etc.
Classification: LCC BS2785.52 .G53 2022 (print) | LCC BS2785.52 (ebook) | DDC 227/.9106—dc23/eng/20220627
LC record available at https://lccn.loc.gov/2022011826
LC ebook record available at https://lccn.loc.gov/2022011827

Crossway is a publishing ministry of Good News Publishers.

VP				31	30	29	28	27	26	25	24	23	22
15	14	13	12	11	10	9	8	7	6	5	4	3	2	1

For
Trinity Church, Aberdeen

Truth be told . . . the one thing in this world I want more than anything else is a great big crowbar, to jimmy myself open and take whatever creature that's sitting inside and shake it clean like a rug and then rinse it in a cold, clear lake . . . and then I want to put it under the sun to let it heal and dry and grow and sit and come to consciousness again with a clear and quiet mind.

DOUGLAS COUPLAND, *MISS WYOMING*

Contents

Preface

COMPLETE. INTACT. UNBROKEN. UNDIVIDED. WHOLE. I'm sure you'll agree that there is something very attractive about these words. Even just sitting there alone on the page without any context they manage to convey health and fullness. They depict how things are meant to be.

And I suspect that you, like me, would love these words to be true of you.

The Bible has different ways of describing what goes on inside us at the deepest level of our beings. There's the word *conscience*, for instance, the part of us that knows what it is to be either clean or dirty on the inside. A further inner world is conveyed by the word *heart*. It portrays the seat of our personalities and the sum total of our internal motivating engine.

I want to take you on a guided tour through one Bible book's penetrating analysis of another internal condition we each live with: "double-mindedness," as diagnosed in the epistle of James.

We know what it's like to be in two minds about something. We've all stood in a shop trying to choose between pairs of shoes, or coats, or new phones. We weigh up big decisions all the time in choosing between alternatives: a school, a house, a career. This is normal. It's what it means to be finite creatures with incomplete knowledge of the ultimate good as we feel our way forward on the path of life.

But the fact that we are capable of going in more than one direction has a darker hue when it comes to our character. Everyone reading these lines will know what it is like to say and do things that can leave us on the other side of our words and actions utterly bewildered about where those choices came from. How could we have been so stupid, so selfish? What on earth made us speak like that? Creatures made in God's image we may be, but sin renders us absurd even to ourselves.

Digging deeper, we know that no one else can see what goes on inside our heads, and so we live with truths about us that only we can comprehend. We are the solitary observers of our inner closed-circuit TV. Sometimes this means there are things we are anxious to keep hidden. Often it means there are things we love which somehow say more about the real us than others can discern on the surface. Always it means there is a kind of fault line running through our personalities, a fracture at our core, which means that what we project is not the full story. We are so often less than who we wish we were.

According to the Bible, we are split down the middle.

So, I want to introduce you to James's painful-but-profound medicine for healing the divided heart. It is a lovingly prescribed course in wholeness. Not just "spiritual" wholeness, as if the spiritual side of our lives were separate from the physical, emotional, or relational aspects of who we are. The picture James paints is one that integrates every part of our lives, before God and in relationship with others. He portrays a Christian life of beauty and moral fitness, a cohesive uprightness to our character, that displays the glory and goodness of God to those around us. It is profoundly attractive, and I want to captivate you as you gaze.

Make no mistake, James's words can cut like a knife. But he is only ever wounding in order to heal. This beautiful book in the Bible can put us together again and lead us part of the way back to who we were always meant to be.

See how God pulls us apart in order to make us whole.

Acknowledgments

THE EPISTLE OF JAMES has long been a perplexing book for me. On the one hand, James writes with a disarming simplicity of command and exhortation that is hard to sidestep or misunderstand; on the other, my logical mind has always struggled to perceive a distinctive wavelength or to trace a consistent argument from start to end. So, what you hold in your hands is my own attempt to wrestle with a portion of Holy Scripture which speaks a language we know, but in an accent that nevertheless sometimes leaves us unsure.

If there is any coherence to these pages—and if in God's kindness you gain from them any light for the journey—then it is entirely down to an array of people who have wrestled with James before and alongside me, to outstanding commentaries, books, and sermons that instructed me on the way, and to friends and family who helped me as I wrote and thought.

First and foremost, I am indebted to Dr. Andy Gemmill and his fresh and illuminating work on James. I have heard him speak on this book in many different contexts over the years, and the architecture of my approach has been profoundly shaped by his clear thinking, his own personal and pastoral engagement with the sharp end of James's words, and his gift for penetrating application. His is the blueprint; mine is the attempt to fill in and elaborate as many details as I can. I am very grateful for his constructive comments and preacher's eyes on my material.

My friend Ben Traynor preached James with me and opened up parts of it vividly for us at Trinity Church in Aberdeen. I am grateful for his permission to include some of his thinking here. Our staff team and elders enabled me to write, either by taking on parts of my work at different points or by offering feedback on earlier drafts. I am very grateful to Will Allan, Simon Barker, Nicola Fitch, and Drew Tulloch. Our ministry trainees and others worked with me on the questions for discussion and personal reflection that appear at the end of each chapter, and the whole book is the better for their input. My thanks to Alex Hanna, Hannah McEwan, Sam Moore, James Shrimpton, Sam Williams, and Struan Yarney. Nothing would ever have materialized without the skill and support of Eleanor Trotter and Caleb Woodbridge (IVP), and Justin Taylor and Anthony Gosling (Crossway). They all provided kind encouragement and wisdom at every step along the way.

As always, it was my own family who made everything possible. My wonderful parents picked up the slack more times than I can count, and certainly more than they will ever say. I owe thanks to my brother, Jonathan, for his excellent suggestions. My wife, Angela, and our children, Archie, Ella, Sam, and Lily, regularly went without me while I tried to write a bit here and there, and even packed me off to the remote Culfosie Cottage in Strathdon (courtesy of the kindness of Phil and Philippa Mason). I'd like to think it's a sacrifice they made to see the book finished, but I am quite sure life is just generally easier all round without me!

In this our eighteenth year in Aberdeen, I want to dedicate this book to the church family I am privileged to serve at Trinity. These precious brothers and sisters first heard what is printed here in sermon form. As always, they received these faltering efforts with humility and grace, and with patient and attentive listening. It is one of my great joys in our shared life to be seeking to grow in the grace of the Lord Jesus together, until we are made whole forever in a world made new. "Blessed is the man who remains steadfast under trial, for when he has stood the test he will receive the crown of life, which God has promised to those who love him" (James 1:12).

Introduction

Getting Your Bearings

You have to bite the hand that reads you.

TINA BROWN, QUOTED IN *THE WEEK*

WHY IS UNFAITHFULNESS such an undoing? In a world of casual sex, and where pornography is readily available to be consumed on a massive scale, it remains a surprising fact that adultery is rather taboo. It is as though we have thrown a precious item under the bus (sex), but we have kept the price tag in our hearts (faithfulness). Something about breaking a promise and trashing a covenant still seems to stand out to everyone as being obviously damaging. In our culture's eyes it is not that sex with multiple partners is wrong per se. But if it happens in violation of the assurances of loyalty that we have given to someone else, then we seem to know deep inside that something has gone awry.

Sexual unfaithfulness can devastate like few things on earth. Our very identity is at stake in the delicate connection between what we promise with our words and what we do with our bodies, such that infidelity shatters trust between people and can destroy the self-worth of each individual involved. It divides that which is not meant to be divided.

Unfaithfulness is such a catastrophic undoing because it strikes at the very heart of who we are meant to be as people: whole, committed, united to God, and united to others in faithful relationship. This is why, from start to finish, the Bible is the story of a marriage, God's marriage with his people, with human marriage given to us as a real, lived-out illustration of God's relationship with us.

The story of the first marriage in the Bible, in Genesis 2:24, is retold by the apostle Paul not only to instruct husbands and wives how to love each other but also to communicate how God loves us: "'Therefore a man shall leave his father and mother and hold fast to his wife, and the two shall become one flesh.' This mystery is profound, and I am saying that it refers to Christ and the church" (Eph. 5:31–32). It is simply astonishing that the physical, sexual intimacy of husband and wife is given to us as the analogy of how close we are to Jesus in his saving love for us. That act creates a oneness out of twoness. It's why Paul can say, "He who loves his wife loves himself" (Eph. 5:28). Just as Jesus loves us in such a profound way that we become members of his body, so too the joining of a man and woman in marriage means that there is no longer a "he" without a "she," or a "her" without a "him." Ray Ortlund notes that the original marriage of Adam and Eve was based on the fact that the woman was made "out of the very flesh of the man, so that the bond of marriage reunites what was originally and literally one flesh."[1] Two become one new whole, and they are to remain whole.

This reality of human love in marriage as an illustration of divine love in our union with Christ is why the Bible uses the severing of marriage in adultery as a powerful image of what we do to God in our sin. What God desires is our oneness with him in love, and wholehearted obedience flowing from that love, but what we return to him instead, in our rebellion, is our love of someone or something else alongside or instead of him. The fundamental problem of the human condition is not primarily what we say or do; rather, it is who and what we love instead of God. He is the husband of his people (Isa. 54:5; Ezek. 16:8–14), but we are his adulterous people in return (Num. 15:39; Ps. 106:39; Ezek. 23:20).

In this book I suggest that the epistle of James shows this essence of our sin in crystal clear terms. James is deeply in tune with the Bible's story of God's own people prostituting themselves with other lovers. Instead of being wholly devoted lovers of God and fully integrated lovers of others, God's people can be so deeply divided that James will cry out, "You adulterous people!" (4:4). This is precisely what makes his letter so painful, and yet his clear sight is also, of course, what makes it so full of grace and hope. James has a beautiful conception of what life should be like when lived out of love for God and love for others, so his cutting words are merely flowing from his profound sense of how different things could be. He has such a clear vision of the good life that when he sees its ugly opposite, he cannot beat about the bush, but simply calls it out for what it is. We always think we want the truth, but actually *hearing* the truth is usually much more difficult.

The first thing to learn as we walk the road of becoming whole with James is that it involves him telling, and our accepting, the truth about ourselves.

In what follows, I work from the assumption that James is so preoccupied with the theme of wholeness that we will find it running through every single part of his letter like a golden thread. He is so taken with this idea that it is present at the level of a controlling motif and underlying argument, shaping everything, even when he's not using specific words for wholeness or oneness. It is his governing and unifying theme.

Stand Back and See the Whole

Down through the years, many commentators and preachers have got lost in James, in part, I think, because they have moved through its various details and twists and turns without a clear sense of the entire epistle. The letter seems to bounce from one topic to another. Martin Luther accused James of "throwing things together chaotically."[2] One minute we're reading about trials and testing (1:2–3), then we're thinking about the rich and the poor (1:9–10), then we're back to trials again (1:12). What is James getting at? In fact, James frustrated Luther so much that he went as far as to say that James is "a right strawy epistle" which "has nothing of the nature of the gospel about it."[3] This was largely because of James's words "You see that a person is justified by works and not by faith alone" (2:24). The apostle Paul teaches us justification by faith alone, and here is James flatly contradicting him, right? For Luther, James mangles Scripture.

This apparent clash between Paul and James has been taken by some to represent a conflict between "Pauline Christianity" and "Jewish Christianity." In 1894, Adolf Jülicher called James "the least Christian book of the New Testament," and more recently James Dunn regarded James as "the most Jewish, the most undistinctively Christian document in the New Testament."[4]

All of this unease might sound strange to you. Many of us love James for its simplicity. It is such a practical letter, without too much tough theology to wrap our heads around. Maybe Romans is for the left-brained people who like linear logic, but James is for the right-brained artistic people who think in pictures. "If we put bits into the mouths of horses so that they obey us, we guide their whole bodies as well. Look at the ships also . . ." (James 3:3–4). It's so vivid, and we understand it straight away.

At the outset, however, I need to say very clearly that Martin Luther was wrong. James is not worthless, and I want to show you why not. He does not contradict Paul, and we're going to see how and why. It is also a wonderfully Christian book in its Jewishness. I agree with Richard Bauckham when he says in his superb study that James's relationship to Judaism simply parallels Jesus's relationship to Judaism.[5] In other words, if James is "undistinctively Christian," then so is Jesus himself. We will find some of the greatest riches in the book precisely because of their closeness to the teaching of the Lord Jesus, and it is he, of course, who is the true and ultimate fulfillment of Judaism's oldest promises in the Scriptures and its greatest hopes for the Messiah and his new world order.

The opening verses suggest that James's epistle was probably meant to be a round-robin letter to various churches in Asia Minor: "the twelve tribes in the Dispersion." This is obviously a reference to the twelve tribes of Israel, but it's also clear that James is writing to those Jews who confess Jesus as the Messiah. Thus, they were very likely to be Jewish Christians who lived outside the land of promise, those who had been dispersed from their ancient religious landmarks, such as Jerusalem. Douglas Moo suggests that the fact that these Jewish believers in Jesus the Messiah had been forced to live away from their home country explains a "major characteristic of the readers of the letter: their poverty and oppressed condition."[6] At the same time, Moo notes, although "the situation of the church in the world provides one important context for the letter . . . the letter ultimately has much more to say about the problem of the world getting into the church."[7]

That is a nice turn of phrase. Notice how it focuses our attention on the idea of mixing two things that should not be mixed (church and world). It directs us to the seriousness of James's tone and the pointed urgency with which he writes. So, I want to side very clearly with those who say that this is a wonderfully practical letter, but then I also want to ask, "Are we sitting comfortably?"

We are in for a very painful ride. Very painful indeed.

For James is a letter written to churches in danger of dying, churches that could become very sick. James knows that the recipients could embark on a one-way journey to the morgue. This means he will quickly blow out of the water any ideas we might have that this is a lovely letter full of "how-to" tips and nice, simple rules for life. Rather, the words in James are what you get when you go to the doctor and say, "Look, I've got this cough, but I'm sure it's nothing really." You're examined and scanned, and then a message arrives urging you to schedule an appointment. The doctor says to you: "Now about that cough: it's a symptom of a much bigger problem. I've got some bad news. You have a deadly disease."

I want to show you that James is like the best of physicians in three ways: he sees symptoms, he diagnoses the underlying disease, and he knows exactly which medicine we need to take.

Observe the Symptoms

James is writing to churches that could soon be on their deathbeds unless they take drastic action; they are fellowships containing men and women behaving badly. And when we look at a church that is going so badly wrong, it needs to serve as a warning to us too. It is the measure of God's kindness to us that sometimes he puts the cadaver on the slab, cuts it open, and tells us to have a look at what killed this once living, breathing organism, so that we can take action to prevent it from happening to us too.

Maybe, as you read these lines, your fellowship is not the kind of church that is facing some of these drastic situations. Indeed, I hope your fellowship is healthy and thriving. If so, it is so important for us to listen to James's words now, before trouble comes. Good health is like that, isn't it? We don't really notice it until it's gone. It's what older people say as they succumb to frailty and weakness: "Oh, I wish I'd appreciated the health of my youth." It's what someone says after the terrible diagnosis: "I just didn't know I was living; my health was the best thing I had, and now it's gone." It's what we all said as the coronavirus pandemic turned our worlds upside down in 2020, and we realized how much we had been taking for granted, unthinkingly. Suddenly, 2019 was the best year that ever was.

But not everyone reading this will be on the mountaintop. It is possible that you have recently come through, or are still experiencing, the ugly and upsetting seasons that can roll into a church's life. They are so very common, and most fellowships face times of tension at some point. Maybe you are hurting right now from the reality of sin working its way through relationships you hold dear and harming a church family you have cherished for many years. You might need the Lord's help to forgive and to embark on a new path of spiritual wholeness. Some of us may need to be honest and admit that we've even played a part in things going off the rails.

Here are three symptoms of what is going wrong in the churches to whom James is writing.

Symptom 1: These Churches Are Speaking Angry Words

We get the first hint of angry words within the church very early on: "Know this, my beloved brothers: let every person be quick to hear, slow to speak, slow to anger" (James 1:19). This is amplified a few verses later: "If anyone thinks he is religious and does not bridle his tongue but deceives his heart, this person's religion is worthless" (1:26). The sense that a lot of problems in this letter revolve around our speech becomes crystal clear in chapter 3: "And the tongue is a fire, a world of unrighteousness" (3:6). James is writing because he knows it ought not to be so, but, in fact, it is so. For these believers, the tongue is a world of trouble.

Do you know what this is like? Fights, quarrels, and words that ignite and explode and harm and hurt? Of course you do.

I am grateful for the perceptive words of Andy Crouch that one of the great gifts of families at their best is that there we discover what fools we are. "No matter how big your house, it's not big enough to hide your foolishness from people who live with you day after day."[8]

For the Gibson family, foolishness always seems to reach epic proportions on Thursdays. I don't know what it is about Thursdays. I call them TTT: Tongue-Torched Thursdays. Maybe it's because, for me as a minister, by that point my work is beginning to funnel down toward Sunday, and I'm starting to feel the pressure of all the things left to be done before there's any semblance of a coherent sermon. My wife has finished her part-time work for the National Health Service and is feeling tired. Our kids all seem to wake up cranky on Thursday mornings.

With alarming regularity, we manage to arrive at the breakfast table with short fuses and barely concealed irritation. Then someone casts a look deliberately designed to wind up someone else. There follows a condescending action, usually involving cereal bowls, spoons, and milk, or hairclips or lunch boxes—and out it comes, sibling to sibling, husband to wife, parent to child. The words are sharp. The touch paper is lit. The dog is bemused. And we're off to the races. Again.

We all know what it's like to try to tame the tongue. But do you know what James is saying to us here? Don't bother. You won't do it. It can't be done. Now, don't get him wrong. James doesn't mean we don't need to change our speech, nor does he mean that speaking in these awful ways is an acceptable minor blip. No, his point is that soap in our mouths won't solve the real problem. The sinful speech is just a symptom; it's not the disease.

We'll soon come to the deeper problem, but first, two other symptoms.

Symptom 2: These Churches Are Drawing Ugly Lines

"My brothers, show no partiality as you hold the faith in our Lord Jesus Christ, the Lord of glory" (James 2:1). It's obvious from the opening verses of chapter 2 that James's first readers needed to be warned against drawing lines between those who had money and those who did not. They were honoring certain types of people and dishonoring others. There was an "in" crowd and an "out" crowd: an attraction to the people with means, wealth, and status and an overlooking of the poor, marginalized, and downtrodden. Haves and have nots.

This kind of demarcation within the walls of God's family is an ugly aberration and a downright denial of the gospel of grace: "Listen, my beloved brothers, has not God chosen those who are poor in the world to be rich in faith and heirs of the kingdom, which he has promised to those who love him?" (2:5).

So, this letter is going to ask us to reflect on the price tags we attach to people as we experience church together. It is going to be an uncomfortable examination of whether our whole way of assigning value and worth is actually distinct from the world in which we live or merely an uncritical aping of it.

Symptom 3: These Churches Are Not Doing Good Works

"What good is it, my brothers, if someone says he has faith but does not have works? Can that faith save him?" (James 2:14).

Here is why I think the letter of James is so challenging for the evangelical church. James is writing to a church that has faith, one that loves the gospel. The theology on offer in its worship services is orthodox, the doctrinal precision second to none. This is a church that loves preaching. Its members love the Bible. Yes, they love hearing it, *but they don't do what it says* (1:22). And so James writes with a very stark prognosis indeed: no good works, then actually no living faith. You're dead. "For as the body apart from the spirit is dead, so also faith apart from works is dead" (2:26).

When I was little and visited the doctor, I remember being asked to stick out my tongue. Here James is essentially doing the exam: "Let me take a good look at you. Let me examine you and listen to you." And what he hears are explosive words; what he sees are ugly lines and an absence of good deeds.

So, those are the symptoms. What's the cure?

Please observe what James *doesn't* say. He never says that the cure is simply this: speak good words, don't draw lines, and do good deeds.

No. "Rather," says James, in effect, "hop off the table and come and take a seat, for I need to speak to you. Let's park your symptoms. They're not your real problem. They have triggered one huge warning light. You have a deadly disease."

Diagnose the Disease

See if you can spot the diagnosis:

> If any of you lacks wisdom, let him ask God, who gives gener-
> ously to all without reproach, and it will be given him. But let
> him ask in faith, with no doubting, for the one who doubts is
> like a wave of the sea that is driven and tossed by the wind. For
> that person must not suppose that he will receive anything from
> the Lord; he is a double-minded man, unstable in all his ways.
> (James 1:5–8)

The reason why I'm using the medical term *diagnosis* is that James's
analysis of the human condition probes beneath the surface to the
deepest motivating factors of the human psyche. His judgment is
that there is a terrible affliction called double-mindedness (1:8).
The Greek word is *dipsychos*, which literally means "two-souled."
In fact, it seems to be a word that James himself has invented. It's
his own inspired attempt to convey the terrible opposite of what
we are meant to be as children of God: wholehearted, consistent,
shot through with integrity. As Moo observes, it's James's way of
expressing what in other places the Bible considers the tragedy of
the "divided heart."[9]

King David says,

> Everyone utters lies to his neighbor;
>   with flattering lips and a double heart they speak. (Ps. 12:2)

This inner duplicity is why Solomon has to entreat the people in his
benediction at the dedication of the temple: "Let your heart therefore

be *wholly* true to the LORD our God, walking in his statutes and keeping his commandments, as at this day" (1 Kings 8:61). Back in the Psalms again, David petitions God with the same request:

> May integrity and uprightness preserve me,
>> for I wait for you. (Ps. 25:21)

We discover that

> blessed are those who keep his testimonies,
>> who seek him with their *whole* heart. (Ps. 119:2)

Now, if you're reading closely, you will have noticed that James uses the word "double-*minded*," but I have crossed over into speaking about the *heart*. This is key to realizing that James is working not only with discrete words as he tackles the problem of wholeness but also with a profound understanding of the human condition which is deeply immersed in the storyline of the Bible. For, in Scripture, *heart* is the word for the operational headquarters of the human being. Says Craig Troxel, "Everything we think, desire, choose, and live out is generated from this one 'controlling source' and is governed from this one point."[10] Notice the connections in that quotation between mind, desire, and will. Each flows from one directing stream: the heart.

In his wonderful book *With All Your Heart*, Troxel unpacks a rich seam of Puritan theology that operated with a threefold cardiology of mind, desires, and will. He argues that in the Bible the heart is presented

> as a trinity of spiritual functions. . . . The heart includes what we *know* (our knowledge, thoughts, intentions, ideas, meditation,

memory, imagination), what we *love* (what we want, seek, feel, yearn for), and what we *choose* (whether we will resist or submit, whether we will be weak or strong, whether we will say yes or no).[11]

Very simply, this means that James is able to see doubleness across the full panoply of our human condition: in how we think, in whom we love, and in what we do. It comes out in whom we speak to and how we speak to them; it surfaces in a theological confession that is undermined by our lack of practical outworking; it is present in our impatience in suffering as we reveal our inability to wait for the Lord, the righteous Judge. As Richard Bauckham says, the reason why the prayers of the double-minded are not answered is that such people "vacillate between trusting God and looking elsewhere. They do not truly, wholeheartedly, want what they ask of God."[12]

So, I simply want us now to take in James's overall idea that it is possible to have a *twoness* inside us corrupting our oneness. We know that living with two of you can land you on the psychiatrist's couch; as she listens to you describe yourself, and you are eventually given the diagnosis of split personality. James is saying that our deepest problem, the well from which all the symptoms flow, is a spiritual split personality: we are divided on the *inside*, which is what leads us to cause divisions on the *outside*.

So, a divided heart leads to divided actions.[13]

Living as Two

Just look at how doubleness inside us takes shape outside us:

- "But be doers of the word, and not hearers only, deceiving yourselves" (James 1:22). We can be divided between listening and acting. We love to hear, but we don't find it so easy to do. We split them off one from the other. We like being in church and we love the sermon, but by Tuesday we're struggling (again) to do what God told us to do. Why?

- "My brothers, show no partiality as you hold the faith in our Lord Jesus Christ, the Lord of glory" (2:1). James is probing a very profound reason why we honor the rich over the poor. It's because one part of us loves the Lord Jesus Christ, the Lord of glory, and another part of us loves the glory of wealth, riches, and prestige. James is calling his readers not to be divided in our glory gaze.

- "If a brother or sister is poorly clothed and lacking in daily food, and one of you says to them, 'Go in peace, be warmed and filled,' without giving them the things needed for the body, what good is that?" (2:15–16). We divide faith and good works, thinking we can separate them and safely have one without the presence of the other. Why?

- "From the same mouth come blessing and cursing" (3:10). Notice that the dividing line splits our mouth. Our speech is not united: it is double in form and content.

The World in the Church

We can see, then, that this letter is all about the problem of doubleness where God intends there to be oneness. Its main thesis is that there is no point ever trying to fix the tongue or to change the lines we draw without changing the heart, the source of it all. We will never change how we relate to a poor person and a rich person in the same room unless we realize that the real issue is not money but the evil inside us: "Have you not then made distinctions among yourselves and become judges with evil thoughts?" (James 2:4).

Evil *thoughts* and selfish *desires* are our real problem, the kind willing even to ignore the damage done to the whole body if we can stand to benefit personally. So, James is doing more than giving us a sterile medical term for our problem. In fact, looping back to the start, he calls it adultery, the ultimate form of doubleness, a twisted twoness where there is meant to be beautiful oneness: "You adulterous people! Do you not know that friendship with the world is enmity with God?" (4:4).

Imagine a young couple just returned from their honeymoon. They are starting their life together, a new adventure, and the doorbell rings. They open it to find an old flame of the husband from years ago. "Hi," she says. "I thought I'd come and live with you for a few years!"

Before the bride can express her astonishment, the husband bounds along, hugs the woman, and exclaims, "This is going to be so much fun! One big happy family!"

Oh, dear! Why is the bride weeping? Because of jealousy. Righteous jealousy. It's because of real love, true love. "Or do you suppose it is to no purpose that the Scripture says, 'He yearns jealously over the spirit that he has made to dwell in us'?" (4:5). Verses like this show us that God is a God of wholeness, of oneness. He hates that things meant to be whole become separate, because this goes against who he is. Remember James's words: "For that person must not suppose that he will receive anything from the Lord; he is a double-minded man, unstable in all his ways" (1:7–8). Such a person cannot receive anything from the Lord, precisely because the Lord himself is not divided. The Lord Jesus was the ultimate whole human being, the one true man whose heart was wholly true to his heavenly Father. Integrity and uprightness preserved him in all that he did; he kept each and every one of God's statutes and commandments. Without fail, he sought God with his whole heart (John 6:38; Heb. 10:5–7).

We will return to the significance of who Jesus is in contrast to who we are. But for now, we simply need to grasp the stinging charge that James is laying at the door of the first hearers: you like someone else in bed; you like being married to the world as well. The world likes the rich over the poor; it quarrels, fights, and murders; it harbors bitter jealousy and selfish ambition.

And when God's people live like that, it shows we are in bed with the world, two-faced in our loves.

So, What Do You Really Believe?

Here is where I find the message of James so penetrating. He is basically saying to us, "The quarreling, the unbridled tongue, the discrimination in our midst—and there are many other symptoms of sickness—reveal that we're happy to cheat on God."

"Yes, Lord, I'm all for you!" we say. Then out come the words, the actions, and the decisions that show I am also all for *me*.

This is a most painful letter. As my friend Andy Gemmill has put it, "James is the kind of physician who can look at our speech and our living and the way we relate to each other, and he can read off those actions what we really believe about God."[14]

Just like a doctor can look at the rash, hear the cough, then listen to the erratic breathing and say, "I'm afraid there's actually a very big problem here," so it's as if James is saying: "Give me a few months among you as a church family. Let me observe and listen. And I will tell you whom you love." He elaborates: "Let me just watch how you treat your friends and speak to your church family and your children, and I will tell you where your heart is. Let me watch you welcome the outsider, and I will tell you what you believe about God." It's that sharp.

So, imagine you're doing a church building project (as we are at Trinity at the time of writing), and you're short of money. A poor man and a rich man arrive in your congregation. After church, James gently takes you aside and points out how he noticed that you spent a lot more time talking to the rich man than to the poor man. Why was that? As you stammer for an answer, James essentially says, "I'll tell you why: it's because you don't believe that God has chosen the poor in the world to be heirs of the kingdom (see 2:5). You don't really believe that." As you falter again, James says, "I will show you my faith by my works" (2:18). For what does it profit a church to gain a whole new building, yet forfeit its own soul?

If all these symptoms point to a deadly disease, then, thankfully, all is not lost. Help is at hand, and it comes from God himself, the great physician.

Receive the Medicine

Churches drop dead, eventually, after years of saying, "That's just the way it is." If you want to kill the gospel in your home, with your kids, in your marriage, you kill it by saying: "Oh well, that's just Thursdays. We're all a bit tired. That's just the way it goes, I suppose."

In fact, the person whose manner is brusque and whose tongue is like a knife needs to change. We should never, as people who love the gospel, say, "That's just the way it is." No, the symptoms are a sign that something is terribly wrong. The tongue can do immense damage. The lack of good works can show your faith to be dead.

So, what do we do with the double mind, the divided heart, the fractured self?

The answer is that there is medicine we can take, called God's grace. "But he gives more grace. Therefore it says, 'God opposes the proud but gives grace to the humble'" (James 4:6). The medicine is repentance: regular, daily, heartfelt turning around and running back to God again. It is learning a new language. We stop saying, "It's just Thursdays," and we start saying, "It's just sin."

Isn't that what James is doing here? "Draw near to God, and he will draw near to you. Cleanse your hands, you sinners, and purify your hearts, you double-minded" (4:8). James speaks plainly. He doesn't use all the tidy euphemisms we use to justify ourselves. Sin is why we honor the rich over the poor, why we speak the way we do, why we can ask others how they are with no intention of ever meeting their needs.

Healing for Fractured Hearts

James teaches us to learn to dig deeper with God. Learn to ask, "What's going on in my heart?" If the language of sin, grace, and forgiveness is not the regular currency of your dinner table, your pillow talk, and your coffee time, and if there are brothers and sisters in your church who have wronged you, or have been wronged by you, and you are not keeping short accounts with one another, let James help.

You heal the divided heart with the gospel. With grace. When was the last time you asked someone to forgive you, the last time you repented out loud to God for your specific thoughts, words, or actions? That's how we measure whether or not we're taking the medicine. And we can start now, wherever we are.

God is so tender with us, so merciful, so patient. Think how jilted lovers act. When someone discovers adultery, what happens?

There's always anger, and then there's the cold shoulder and the bitter exclusion. The days of welcome, warmth, and intimacy are over. Almost inevitably, separation is followed by divorce. But what does God do? "You adulterous people! . . . Draw near to God" (4:4, 8)! Imagine being cheated on and, in response, gently wooing the one who jilted you by saying, "Come close"! James wants us to meet this God afresh.

The grace of God is sweet, sweet medicine. We're going to explore its incredible depths and glorious riches. Grace can make the wounded whole. It can heal the divided heart.

Questions for Discussion or Personal Reflection

1. What are your impressions of the book of James so far?

2. What is meant by the term "double-minded"? Explain it in your own words.

3. Are you able to diagnose the symptoms of your divided heart?

4. How does God calling us to "draw near" give us hope?

5. As you begin this book, what are you most hoping to receive from the letter of James?

1

Perfection

If you want to build a ship, don't drum up people to collect
wood and don't assign them tasks and work, but rather
teach them to long for the endless immensity of the sea.
ANTONIE DE SAINT-EXUPÉRY, *THE WISDOM OF THE SANDS*

[1] James, a servant of God and of the Lord Jesus Christ,

To the twelve tribes in the Dispersion:

Greetings.

[2] Count it all joy, my brothers, when you meet trials of various kinds, [3] for you know that the testing of your faith produces steadfastness. [4] And let steadfastness have its full effect, that you may be perfect and complete, lacking in nothing.

[5] If any of you lacks wisdom, let him ask God, who gives generously to all without reproach, and it will be given him. [6] But let him ask in faith, with no doubting, for the one who doubts is like a wave of the sea that is driven and tossed by the wind. [7] For that person must not suppose that he will receive anything from the Lord; [8] he is a double-minded man, unstable in all his ways.

[9] Let the lowly brother boast in his exaltation, [10] and the rich in his humiliation, because like a flower of the grass he will pass away. [11] For the sun rises with its scorching heat and withers the

grass; its flower falls, and its beauty perishes. So also will the rich man fade away in the midst of his pursuits.

[12] Blessed is the man who remains steadfast under trial, for when he has stood the test he will receive the crown of life, which God has promised to those who love him. [13] Let no one say when he is tempted, "I am being tempted by God," for God cannot be tempted with evil, and he himself tempts no one. [14] But each person is tempted when he is lured and enticed by his own desire. [15] Then desire when it has conceived gives birth to sin, and sin when it is fully grown brings forth death.

[16] Do not be deceived, my beloved brothers. [17] Every good gift and every perfect gift is from above, coming down from the Father of lights, with whom there is no variation or shadow due to change. [18] Of his own will he brought us forth by the word of truth, that we should be a kind of firstfruits of his creatures.

JAMES 1:1–18

I'M TOLD THAT, every summer, the residents of Oxford and Cambridge get a visual treat. They observe tourists trying to board punts on their famous rivers. And nearly always they witness some poor, unsuspecting person doing the splits. It turns out that boarding a boat from dry land is more difficult than many suspect. One leg stays and the other leg goes, and the result is both painful and undignified.

This is James's mental picture of the Christians he is writing to. He can see them with one foot firmly planted in the Bible and with God. But he can also see them with the other foot still touching down in the world, with its ways of thinking, speaking, and acting. And a foot in two totally different domains is no basis for anything stable or whole.

All of Me for All of You

Richard Bauckham comments that in this opening section of his letter, James intends "to highlight the overarching theme of the whole work: perfection."[1] James 1:1–18 is a collection of wisdom sayings, or aphorisms, laid out, it seems, in almost random order. In fact, James is simply highlighting virtually every topic that he will go on to expound in greater detail in the rest of his letter. And he begins by telling us there's a way for us to be "perfect and complete, lacking in nothing" (1:4).

How I would love to be perfect! It's a tantalizing goal for every Christian, and it would be amazing to get there. My wife would love it if I were perfect. My kids would be over the moon. Think how much everyone around me would benefit if I were the complete package, the real deal, in every single area of life. I believe that James begins his letter in this way because, right from the start, he is showing us the opposite of being double-minded. Being "perfect" is his word for being whole.

"Perfect" is translated from the Greek word *teleios*, and in fact it appears twice in verse 4: "And let steadfastness have its *full* [*perfect*] effect, that you may be *perfect*." James reinforces this with a very similar word, *holoklēros*, "complete," and with the extra phrase "lacking in nothing" (1:4). Bauckham points out that the *teleios* word group occurs seven times in James; surely this is not accidental, with seven being the number of perfection or completeness in the Jewish Bible. Indeed, in 3:17, James will sum up the "wisdom from above" in seven attributes.[2] As well as appearing twice in 1:4, *teleios* comes again in 1:17, 25; 2:8, 22; and 3:2.

When we struggle to find coherent ordering in James, we may be looking for the wrong thing: the logical flow of an argument you'd find in the apostle Paul's writings and other epistles. But, as I suggested earlier, not finding this in James doesn't mean James is random or illogical. On the contrary, what he is doing instead is presenting us with a worldview deeply immersed in the wisdom tradition of the Old Testament Scriptures, which was itself profoundly informed by God's giving of the law to his people. James has a vision of what God intends for his people—perfection—and every part of his letter is related to this intention. Says Bauckham, "Careful study shows that this is not just one important theme, but the overarching theme of the whole letter, encompassing all the other major concerns."[3]

So, what does James mean by perfection?

Way back in time, when the children of Israel stood on the edge of the promised land, ready to receive their marching orders from Moses, he instructed them to "therefore choose life" (Deut. 30:19). Moses preached a sermon telling God's people they would have more from his hand than they had ever dreamed, and there was a simple way to receive everything he was willing to give. It was a beautiful sermon, known as the *Shema*: "Hear, O Israel: the LORD our God, the LORD is one" (Deut. 6:4). That was point one of the sermon. The Lord is not divided. Many in my congregation wish my sermon points were as brief or as clear as that.

And what comes next in the sermon? Point two: "You shall love the LORD your God with all your heart and with all your soul and with all your might" (Deut. 6:5). The Lord is not divided, and so you should not be divided either. Love him with all of you, love him wholly and completely.[4] As Scott Redd puts it: "God's character is whole, pure, full, rich, and simple, and it demands a response of whole, pure, full, rich, and simple love. Whether public or private, individual or corporate, spiritual or carnal, God's people are to be simply and wholly in love with Him."[5]

Remember that this is a letter to Jewish Christians now scattered throughout the world. They cherished their Hebrew Scriptures and knew the law of Moses inside out. They also knew that because God is one, what he loves is oneness. Yet, as we've seen, James is writing to churches displaying in all their outward factions their inward fractures. Instead of whole hearts, they have divided hearts. They are not yet perfect or complete. Make no mistake, they could say: "I love you, Lord; I really do. I've been born again. I have a love for you that I never used to have. I love your word. I love your law. I love your people. But truth be told, I also still love me. *My* kingdom come. *My* will be done. I am split, double-minded."

So, here we are at the start of this wonderful, stinging, antiseptic letter that is like antibiotics being pumped into our spiritual system to seek out the disease and kill it at its root. Right away James is showing us that his aim is God's aim for his children: perfection. Douglas Moo states, "Nothing less than complete moral integrity will ultimately satisfy the God who is himself holy and righteous, completely set apart from sin."[6]

The Lord Jesus himself told us, "You therefore must be perfect, as your heavenly Father is perfect" (Matt. 5:48). Mature. Complete. Spiritually whole; our splitness refined into oneness. The fact that the Lord Jesus himself expressed the same idea here ties James into the bigger picture of the Bible's storyline. In his brilliant study of the Sermon on the Mount, Jonathan Pennington argues that one of the key ideas—if not *the* key idea—that make the sermon hang together is "wholeness," "completeness," or "singular devotion."[7] When Jesus says that we must be whole or complete as our heavenly Father is whole and complete (Matt. 5:48), this comes after Jesus has outlined six ways in which a "greater righteousness" than that of the scribes and the Pharisees is required in order to enter the kingdom of heaven. The Pharisees are hypocrites because, says Pennington, "they are not unified in heart and action; they actually *do* the right things, but they are not the right kind of people because their hearts are wrong. . . . They are not 'pure in heart' and therefore they cannot see God (Matt. 5:8)."[8]

Such unity of heart and action is most perfectly embodied, of course, in the Lord Jesus himself, who came not to abolish the law that called for singular perfection, but rather to fulfill it (Matt. 5:17). He is the true, perfect, whole, faithful Israelite and, as such, the perfect, whole, and faithful exemplary man. We will see later on that James calls him "the Lord of glory" (2:1). And it is this title for the Lord Jesus that grounds his deeply whole-Bible perspective of the undivided heart, whereby a person gives himself or herself to God, holding nothing back. James has a wonderful vision of human flourishing, flowing from singular devotion to God in his law and his grace.

Three Steps toward Wholeness

Here are three things James tell us to do if we want to be whole.

Think Clearly

If the goal is "that you may be perfect and complete" (James 1:4), let James work backward from that point and show us how we get there. Wholeness is where God is taking us, but how do we reach it? "Let steadfastness have its full effect" (1:4). But how do we achieve steadfastness? We get it by "the testing of [our] faith" (1:3).

So, we can trace the steps along the way to the perfection goal. When we meet "trials of various kinds" (1:2), God is testing our faith to produce steadfastness, and that steadfastness will then lead to wholeness and completeness.

I believe this is one of the big surprises of James's letter. And it's a bit unwelcome too, if we're honest. Just as in the introduction we saw that there is no wholeness without loving truth telling, so here we learn there is no wholeness without soreness. There is no perfection and completeness without suffering trials of various kinds. You may be so used to this idea as a Christian that you haven't paused as you have read the text of James simply to reflect on its strangeness: the road to perfection is the path of pain.

Again, we should consider how closely James's teaching aligns with that of the Lord Jesus in the Sermon on the Mount, where Jesus presents a vision of human wholeness and flourishing that is profoundly paradoxical in nature. It is the poor in spirit, the mourning, the meek, the hungry and thirsty who stand to gain the kingdom and life with God himself. This is what Pennington calls "a rich reservoir of 'black gold.' It is a divine gold of priceless worth, but it appears to be only in darkness." Jesus commends states of being that seem to be profoundly *non*-flourishing in nature.[9]

James shares this perspective: God tests your faith to produce steadfastness, in order to make you perfect and complete. In fact, more than this, again in words similar to those of Jesus in the Beatitudes (Matt. 5:2–11), James promises an encounter with God on the other side of suffering that is truly beautiful: "Blessed is the man who remains steadfast under trial, for when he has stood the test he will receive the crown of life, which God has promised to those who love him" (1:12).

But if we want to reach that point whole and complete, and if we want to receive the crown of life at the end of time, then we need to keep working even further backward, according to the logic of James's argument. For he gives a very significant command in 1:2 which tells us how to view the fiery trials that lead to steadfastness, and which, in turn, lead to perfection. And we won't reach any of those stages if we don't do this first: "Count it all joy, my brothers, when you meet trials of various kinds" (1:2). We have worked all the way back to the very start of his argument, and here is the key command that underpins everything.

If you're like me, I suspect that when trials land in your lap unexpectedly, one of the first things you do is stop thinking and start feeling. But here is James telling us that we need to *think* clearly about our trials. We need to engage our minds. The first thing to do if we want to reach the goal is to think. Another way of saying it is, "Consider it all joy." Reckon it. We are to use clear, rational thought in order to understand how it could be joyful.

Notice that James doesn't say, "*Feel* it all joy." It can happen, but it's rare in my experience for tears to be joyful. Nor does James say, "Consider it *happiness*" when you meet trials. There's a huge difference between happiness and joy. Happiness is circumstantial; it's here one moment and gone the next. But joy is the deep, settled knowledge that God is in this, that nothing he sends me—nothing!—is outside his care and his loving purposes for me.

Notice, too, that you are to count it all joy *when* you meet trials. When, not if. It is certain that if we live long enough in this world, we will suffer. We will be bereaved or cause others to be bereaved. We will enter circumstances that will have the ability to crush us, and yet, says James, there is a way of considering joy in those trials, and it is to realize that God is doing something, working to make us whole.

C. S. Lewis gives the most wonderful illustration of how and why God works like this:

Imagine yourself as a living house. God comes in to rebuild that house. At first, perhaps, you understand what he is doing. He is getting the drains right and stopping the leaks in the roof and so on: you knew that those jobs needed doing and so you are not surprised. But presently he starts knocking the house about in a way that hurts abominably and does not seem to make sense. What on earth is he up to? The explanation is that he is building quite a different house from the one you thought of—throwing out a new wing here, putting on an extra floor there, running up towers, making courtyards. You thought you were going to be made into a decent little cottage; but he is building a palace. He intends to come and live in it himself. . . . If we let him . . . he will make the feeblest and filthiest of us into a . . . dazzling, radiant, immortal creature, pulsating all through with such energy and joy and wisdom and love as we cannot now imagine, a bright stainless mirror which reflects back to God perfectly . . . his own boundless power and delight and goodness. The process will be long and in parts very painful; but that is what we are in for. Nothing less.[10]

If the end product is worth having, then the pain along the way is worth enduring. But it's only if we want to be whole, to have every inner fracture healed, if we want to be mature and perfect and complete, that we will we count trials "all joy" (1:2).

49

Take the athlete who is training, running, pushing for the victor's crown, like the "crown of life" in 1:12. That athlete who wants to turn a dream into reality counts it a joy to train, even if there is pain in the sweat and the tears, because he or she knows what this testing of mental and physical strength is going to achieve. Indeed, the word "steadfastness" in 1:4 takes us directly to the gym because it means "remaining under" something successfully. The bodybuilder remains under the weight of the bench press, facing resistance. This is James's way of saying that just as faith pushes back against the heavy burden, just as the muscle grows under the strain, so faith grows under the trial. But you do that—you keep sweating, pushing, hanging in there—only if you want the end product of the perfect spiritual body.

We know that some of the very best things emerge only after the most painful of experiences. James believes that the essence of Christian wholeness is based on this same principle, as God refines, purifies, tests, and perfects his people.

It's very possible that as you are reading these lines, you are suffering and carrying a heavy load. Maybe others close to you know about it and are taking the strain with you; maybe no one else at all knows, and the sheer loneliness is adding insult to injury. Some of us are meeting the trial of loneliness head-on. For others it's the trial of unemployment, of unfulfilled sexual longing, of bereavement, of long-term sickness, or of disappointment. It's the trial of old age: body creaking, heart aching, friends departing. It's the trial of having to move out of your home in your later years. It's the trial of difficult, tedious, mind-numbing employment. Your faith is being tested in a difficult marriage. Or your children have needs you don't know how to meet. There's the trial of midlife crisis, of middle-aged depression. Or your sexuality is uncertain, your gender identity confusing, and you don't know where to turn.

Whether right now or at some other point in our lives, we will face serious trials. Something will turn up the temperature, and so, like a precious metal being tested in the heat, our faith in God will enter the crucible.

In his commentary on James, R. Kent Hughes cites a beautiful illustration by Richard Seume:

> Life on earth would not be worth much if every source of irritation were removed. Yet most of us rebel against the things that irritate us, and count as a heavy loss what ought to be rich gain. We are told that the oyster is wiser: that when an irritating object, like a bit of sand, gets under the "mantle" of his shell, he simply covers it with the most precious part of his being and makes of it a pearl. The irritation that it was causing is stopped by encrusting it with the pearly formation. A true pearl is therefore simply a victory over irritation. Every irritation that gets into our lives today is an invitation to pearl culture. The more irritations the devil flings at us, the more pearls we may have. We need only to welcome them and cover them completely with love, that most precious part of us, and the irritation will be smothered out as the pearl comes into being. What a store of pearls we may have, if we will![11]

James is writing about God's pearl culture. A pearl is a mature saint, not lacking anything, a perfect and complete believer. But some of us are just starting to get the sand in the eye. We're rubbing it and rubbing it; we want it out. But God is just leaving it there, and so we're rubbing even more furiously. We're wondering where God is and what he is doing, and James is coming alongside here to teach us how God makes pearls. We need to smother the irritation with the most precious part of us, with clear-eyed thinking.

My prayer as you read this is that you might begin to see what God is doing, and what he might be killing in you, and what parts of you he is knocking about in order to put your divided soul back together.

Or you might be a pearl already. I'm sure many of you are. I don't know what difficulties God has already brought you through.

But it's also possible that you haven't yet had much grit in your eyes; your life has gone with the flow so far. Can I encourage you to look around your church with fresh eyes and get to know some pearls? Spend time with them. If you don't know who they are, ask your pastor to introduce you, and learn firsthand how God did some of his deepest work in their lives when no one else was looking.

It is a great mistake to think that when we get it all together, our trials will somehow lessen. That if we get the girl, find the job, pass the exam, or recover from the illness, we will somehow have arrived. No, there are trials of various kinds right until we cross the finish line, until the crown of life is placed on our heads by the Lord Jesus.

Do we want to be whole? Do we long to love God with all our hearts and souls and strength more than anything else in all the world? This question really matters, because if we don't, we will not endure the trials when they come. Trials do exactly what they say on the tin: they test, they probe, they examine, and they ask the genuinely hard questions about what we're really living for.

Ask Boldly

If these words are really hard to read, and your trial feels like you are stuck in a furnace and it is almost unbearable, then James tells us to ask God for the wisdom to see it for what it is. "If any of you lacks wisdom, let him ask God, who gives generously to all without reproach, and it will be given him" (1:5). Experiencing suffering and counting it all joy certainly doesn't come naturally; you need wisdom. But look who you are asking: the God "who gives generously to all without reproach." God is not in heaven with arms folded, scolding you for finding the trial difficult. On the contrary, he is lavish in his help and his generosity overflows if we ask him for the wisdom to see that he is playing the long game, the maturity game.

Here is where a little theology can go a very long way. Just as the word "perfect" is probably better rendered "whole" or "complete" because of James's vision of the undivided person, so too the word "generously" as part of the phrase "God, who gives generously," in 1:5, might best be understood slightly differently. This is the Greek word *haplōs*, and several commentators show that it comes from a root whose basic meaning is "single" or "simple." It is related to verses such as Ephesians 6:5, where, notes Moo, Paul tells slaves to obey their earthly masters "with *sincerity* of heart."[12] Luke Timothy Johnson says that the word "signifies simplicity as opposed to complexity; by extension it signifies a lack of calculation and openness."[13] Here in James it means that God is the one "who gives sincerely, without hesitation or mental reservation," says Peter Davids. "He does not grumble or criticize. His commitment to his people is total and undeserved: they can expect to receive."[14] Other scholars note how James's instruction to ask God, who will give in a *haplōs* manner, is an intentional echo of Jesus's words "Ask, and it will be given to you" (Matt. 7:7). There the emphasis is on the character of the one we petition: he is always ready and willing to give.

But more than this, in Luke 11:34, where Jesus says, "When your eye is *healthy*, your whole body is full of light," he uses a word that is linked to *haplōs*, such that older translations like the King James Version render this as the "*single* eye," Moo comments.[15] Inner health depends on the eye seeing with uprightness, with integrity.

The point is this: words and ideas that we might apply to sincere and undivided *creatures* are actually being used by James in relation to *God*. As Moo says, James has taken a term "denoting 'integrity' and applied it to God. Such a linguistic move makes sense in the light of James' tendency to portray Christian character as a reflection and outgrowth of God's."[16] So, God gives singularly and sincerely in order to create single-minded, sincere-hearted children.

I will tease out the implications of this. At the heart of James 1:1–18 is a fundamental contrast between God, as our Creator and perfect heavenly Father, and us, as creatures shot through with imperfection and sin. God is everything we are not. He is simple, undivided, and whole, and there is nothing about him that lacks integrity. We are partitioned, fractured, double-minded, and capable of being lured into sin by our own sinful desires. When we face trials, one of the main ways we fail to be steadfast is by giving in to temptation and by blaming God for what is happening in our lives (1:13). And when that happens, we need to know that the evil we are grappling with comes from inside us and not from God, for God cannot be tempted by evil (1:13–14). God is pure goodness, unadulterated light; we suffer from a fallenness that pollutes us from head to toe, leading us astray.

My friend Ben Traynor says that in this part of James it is as if Temptation and Desire form an illicit union, and then, before we know it, we meet them in the maternity ward: the fruit of their union is a child called Sin. Many years later Sin herself gives birth to her own child: Death (1:15).[17] But, amazingly, in contrast to these illicit and deadly unions, God also gives birth: he brings forth redeemed creatures within his creation by his "word of truth," whom he calls the "firstfruits" (1:18). It is a profoundly beautiful phrase, as we will see in the next chapter. In a world of division, sin, and death, God has a way of starting again within his created order, with us his children, as an advance sign of his eventual restoration of the whole of creation. One day, wholeness will be present on every side in the new creation. For now, however, God starts with us.

So, the point of this contrast that James is making between God and us, as well as his behavior and ours, is to hold out to us the path of wholeness. It is not fundamentally about saying or doing the right things, or even believing the right things, important as these are, but rather about receiving the gift of wisdom from God, *so that we become like him.* The path to wholeness is the path to imitating God by receiving what he gives us.

This is why the Lord Jesus says, "Blessed are the pure in heart, for they shall see God" (Matt. 5:8). He is referring, primarily, not to moral purity, although that's undoubtedly included, but rather to an integration and singleness of heart over and against a double heart. We cannot see God unless we are like him, and to be like him, we have to be undivided.

Here is where some more deep theology is so beautiful. Theologians talk about the doctrine of "divine simplicity," which teaches that God is a simple being. Used in this way, the word "simple" does not have an intellectual sense, as if God were not mysterious or immense; nor does it mean that his ways are straightforwardly comprehensible to us. Rather, it is being used in the sense of compositional integrity. God is one. He is whole. He is not comprised of parts—different attributes like wisdom, power, and goodness—as if he could dispense with any one of them and yet remain God. No, what God *has* (wisdom, power, goodness, love, and so on), he actually *is*.[18] And everything God has and is, he is perfectly.

Divine perfection is what is known as a "summative attribute," an attribute that characterizes all his other attributes: his wisdom, goodness, and power are *perfect* wisdom, *perfect* goodness, and *perfect* power.[19] Divine simplicity rests on the biblical idea that God is self-existent (Ex. 3:14), and his being and attributes do not depend on anything or anyone else. This is why James says that God is the "Father of lights with whom there is no variation or shadow due to change" (1:17). If God is perfectly wise, good, powerful, loving, and so on, then he cannot ever become more wise, more good, or more powerful, and he cannot ever become less of any of his attributes either. He cannot change because he has no lack to overcome, nor any higher blessedness yet to realize. Who and what God is, he is, perfectly. Nothing *makes* him wise or good or loving; he *is* these qualities because he is who he is.

If this is making your head hurt, then take a step back. James believes that God is a united whole, a being of perfect integrity and oneness, and our greatest problem is that we are not yet like him in our character. We are pulled in different directions, capable of great good and of catastrophic evil, tossed like waves on the sea by the wind. But God is constant, immovably and unchangeably good in who he is and what he gives.

This has wonderfully rich applications for us. Sometimes it is the older theologians who express these things best, not just in terms of depth of understanding but in the beauty of their practical outworkings too. The seventeenth-century Reformed Dutch pastor and theologian Petrus van Mastricht understood exactly what difference this view of God makes to everyday life. He said, based on James 1:5, that because God is "most simple," he gives simply, that is, without division or parts. When God gives, he "gives himself, all that he is, and all his attributes, which, by simplicity, are inseparable—his wisdom, power, goodness and grace—devoting them to us."[20]

This is why James will later tell us, "Draw near to God, and he will draw near to you" (4:8). *He* will draw near, all of him, his person. God doesn't seek to overcome our dividedness by giving us bits of him that we might like to patch up who we are, as if we're doing all right in the "goodness" department but we could do with a bit of a top-up in the "wisdom" department. No, in giving us wisdom when we ask for it, God is actually giving us himself. And so, because of this divine action toward us, Mastricht says, "Let us also then with a simple and whole heart rest in God alone, and because of his integrity and uprightness . . . let us promise him all that is ours (Psalm 25:11)."[21] This is Deuteronomy 6:4–5 in action. There should be a correspondence between who God is and who we are, and this alignment wonderfully expresses James's vision of believers in relation to our Father in heaven.

So, for James, God is our Father and we are his children, and that relationship should express itself in sincere asking. It's really important to know that James's words about asking in faith and not doubting do not mean that all true Christians never have doubts. That is clearly not true. Rather, as it has been said, doubt is faith thinking itself clear. The opposite of faith is not doubt; it is unbelief. We often wrestle with the difficult contours of Christian belief in a painful world. That may be where you are today. It's certainly where many of us are all the time, and where I often am.

What James means here by doubt is amplified in 1:6–8. He has in mind the person who goes with God's wisdom on a Sunday but the world's wisdom on a Monday. That person likes friendship with God on a Tuesday but friendship with the world on a Wednesday. Double-minded people are blown here and there. They cannot give themselves to what God says, or to crying out to him: "Lord, I long to follow you with all my heart. Heal me; help me." Instead, they pick and mix, with a bit of Jesus and a bit of their own thinking. A bit of Bible and a bit of the world. A bit of you, Lord, and a bit—just a bit—of everything else.

Boast Rightly

It is very likely that the greatest trial these believers were facing was that, in their poverty, they were being persecuted by the rich. "But you have dishonored the poor man. Are not the rich the ones who oppress you, and the ones who drag you into court?" (James 2:6). James teaches us that the only way to cope with the trials that come from money, the trials of not having enough or of having too much money, is to boast rightly. "Let the lowly brother boast in his exaltation, and the rich in his humiliation" (1:9–10). If you are lowly, boast in the fact that in God's eyes you are exalted; if you are rich, boast in the gospel that takes you from way up high and puts you down on the same level as everyone else. Boast rightly, in the eternal kingdom, in the crown of life, for "like a flower of the grass [the rich] will pass away. For the sun rises with its scorching heat and withers the grass. . . . So also will the rich man fade away" (1:10–11).

I watched the famous footballer (soccer player) Cristiano Ronaldo on the news recently. He had a huge smile on his handsome, tanned face. "I have everything," he said. "I have everything."

I thought, "Yes, you have everything today, but what about tomorrow?"

Some years ago, I watched the heartrending funeral of George Best, the Manchester United and Northern Ireland legend. He was the greatest footballing superstar of the modern era. Everyone wanted a piece of him, but he was overtaken by the tragedy of alcoholism. Now I have to tell my sons his name. They don't know him. He's gone.

Do you ever find yourself just wishing for a little bit more? Not the lottery, Lord, nothing that obscene—but just a bit more. Enough to be more comfortable, enough not to have to worry—a cushion, a buffer. Enough to get by properly. What we don't consider in these idle wishes is that if money were to take away all the stresses of life, we would just have a new battle to fight in order to see clearly the passing nature of all our riches. When my lowliness does not lead me to boast in the fact that in Jesus God has lifted me up to the heavens and seated me with him there, and when my financial pressure does not lead me to boast in my lowliness, I have one foot in this world and the other in the next. I'm split. When my riches don't lead me to boast in the humbling cross of Christ and things that will last forever, then I might be friends with God, but at the same time I am nurturing my friendship with the world. I'm split.

Let Petrus van Mastricht help us again.

Divine simplicity teaches us to acquiesce to our lot, however simple it may be. For the more simple anything is, the more constant it is, and durable, whereas the more composite, likewise the more dissoluble and corruptible. Thus, God is most immutable because he is most simple, while on the contrary the angels, because they exist with qualities that are distinct from their essence, were able to be corrupted by their sin, and material things are the more corruptible the more composite they are, just as we see if we compare stable chemical elements with substances that are mixed. When it comes to our lot, the exact same is true: the more simple, solid, and the more variegated from composition by wealth, honours, friends, the more mutable, and the more you are distracted by so many objects, the more you are liable to cares and anxieties (Luke 10:41), for the more you possess, the more you can lose. It is thus, on this account, that we should, in godly self-sufficiency, accustom our soul to simplicity, and should substitute, for the variety of things the one God who is most sufficient in every way for all things (Gen. 17:1), who is accordingly for us the one thing necessary (Luke 10:42). So then let us possess him as our lot, with a simple acquiescence, and other things as corollaries (Matt. 6:33), looking to the Apostle, who urges this contentment (1 Tim. 6:6) and lights our way in it with his own example (Phil. 4:11–12).[22]

Questions for Discussion or Personal Reflection

1. How do you feel about the Bible's vision of "perfection" as the goal for every Christian? Try to explain that vision in your own words.

2. Why do we find it so hard to consider the trials of life "all joy" (James 1:2), and what difference does this chapter make to that struggle?

3. How does God as one, simple, and unchanging become the solution to our quest for wholeness?

4. In what ways do you find yourself longing for "a little bit more"?

5. Do you have any personal experience of growth (wholeness) developing through suffering? Can you articulate why and how that happened?

2

Doing

The human race is inquisitive about other people's
lives, but negligent to correct their own.

AUGUSTINE, *CONFESSIONS*

[19] Know this, my beloved brothers: let every person be quick to hear, slow to speak, slow to anger; [20] for the anger of man does not produce the righteousness of God. [21] Therefore put away all filthiness and rampant wickedness and receive with meekness the implanted word, which is able to save your souls.

[22] But be doers of the word, and not hearers only, deceiving yourselves. [23] For if anyone is a hearer of the word and not a doer, he is like a man who looks intently at his natural face in a mirror. [24] For he looks at himself and goes away and at once forgets what he was like. [25] But the one who looks into the perfect law, the law of liberty, and perseveres, being no hearer who forgets but a doer who acts, he will be blessed in his doing.

[26] If anyone thinks he is religious and does not bridle his tongue but deceives his heart, this person's religion is worthless. [27] Religion that is pure and undefiled before God the

Father is this: to visit orphans and widows in their affliction, and to keep oneself unstained from the world.

JAMES 1:19–27

———

JAMES NOW SPEAKS to us directly and lovingly about the problem of our split personalities. We've been wrestling with our genuine love for God and the strong pull in totally different directions. The diagnosis on offer here is very deep because it reaches right into the core of our identities, but there is also a cure on offer that is beautifully simple. There is a way to be whole, one person, inside and outside. And it is all to do with our attitude toward the Bible.

The solution is this: do God's word. Do it. That book sitting there beside you on your desk or on your lap or on your phone: take note of what it says, do what it says, and you will be whole. You will find parts of your personality fusing together, parts of your divided heart coming together, your loves dissolving from two into one. A well-known sports clothing brand tells us to "just do it," and that works as a strikingly simple incentive to get the life you always wanted. James puts it the same way. Just do the Bible.

If you're like me, the word that stands out in the title of this book is "whole." We intuitively sense the beauty of being complete. But because we are looking at James, the word "radically" serves a very important purpose too. It comes from the Latin word *radicalis*, which means "root." Over time, *root* became a metaphor to describe the very origin of a thing, the most fundamental part of it.

We now talk about "root and branch" reform of an institution, and we would call such change "radical" because it is so very comprehensive. James is not interested in superficial wholeness, the kind that comes from a great night's sleep or a relaxing holiday, as nice as these are. His kind of wholeness is root-and-branch radical. He wants to get to its very essence and to startle us with the surprise of how such wholeness comes about.

Life with God is not always easy. Even in some of our joys and triumphs it can be difficult to follow Christ. So, life on the narrow way to glory may not be easy, but neither is it complicated. In essence, it is radically simple: do this and you will live.

You want to get better? Stop smoking. Lose weight. Stop drinking. It might be agonizingly hard, of course, but the right thing to do is simple. And really, in some ways, it is the simplicity that needs to shock us as we look at this passage. As his portrait of a truly flourishing life continues to take shape, James is clear, to quote commentator Richard Bauckham, that "purity of heart is not inactive inwardness. It is the inwardness that is consistently expressed in every action."[1] In this chapter of *Radically Whole* and the next, we will see James focus on action as a way of expressing our single-minded devotion to God: here, focusing specifically on actions in relation to God's word; in the next chapter, focusing specifically on actions in relation to others.

Taking In Three Pictures of God's Word

In these verses there are three clear pictures: what the Bible is, how we should respond to it, and what it does. The Bible is an implanted word; it is a revealing mirror; it is a freeing law. I will sketch the outline of these pictures and then suggest a wide range of applications.

Receive God's Implanted Word

"Therefore put away all filthiness and rampant wickedness and receive with meekness the implanted word, which is able to save your souls" (James 1:21).

Implanting things in the body can save it. The pacemaker to regulate the heart. The plate to fuse the bone. The stent into the artery to allow the blood to flow freely. But did you know that implanting the Bible can save you? The word of God, implanted in your heart, in your bones, in your very being, can save you.

I don't think James is making a general point here about being quick to hear each other's words so that anger doesn't rise up. That is true, of course, and we all know that with two ears and only one mouth, we're meant to use the double set more than the single piece. But here I think James is talking about hearing God's word, because in 1:20 the kind of anger we let overflow doesn't lead to the righteousness of God. So, if we want to be like God, we should "put away all filthiness and rampant wickedness and receive with meekness the implanted word" (1:21). Be quick to hear that word, God's word, "which is able to save your souls" (1:21). You want to have a place in the new creation? You need an implant. You need something living grafted into you, poured into you, rooted in you, planted in you: the word of God. Remember what Jesus said about himself in parable form: "Listen! Behold, a sower went out to sow" (Mark 4:3). He went out to implant.

This means that James is asking us to do an input/output self-evaluation. The verbs required of the believer here are passive: *receive, take, accept* the word; we depend on the input of God's word to us. But what do we love doing instead? Output. It's how we roll: by the output of words, anger, and activity unguided by the necessary input.

Look in God's Revealing Mirror

"But be doers of the word, and not hearers only, deceiving yourselves. For if anyone is a hearer of the word and not a doer, he is like a man who looks intently at his natural face in a mirror" (James 1:22–23). At this point we are meant to notice the deliberate shift from input to output, from hearing to doing.

Many years ago, I had coffee with a man who looked like he'd been dragged through a hedge backward. I didn't know him, and it was the first time we had ever met, but I had to tell him that his sweater was on inside out and back to front. It was very embarrassing. He explained that he and his wife had just had a baby! (I smiled, but I remember still thinking to myself, "Who does that?" It took several years before I was in the same position, and then I knew exactly who does things like that!) Immediately, he turned his sweater the right way out and fixed his appearance. But imagine if my sleep-deprived acquaintance had simply thanked me for my observation and carried on into the rest of his day completely indifferent to how he looked.

Imagine looking in the mirror in the morning and seeing what you're like, seeing what needs fixing: the stubble to be shaved off, the makeup to be applied, or the hair to be combed. Imagine going away and ignoring what the mirror reveals. Who does that? Who listens to the Bible, hears it, understands what God is saying, and goes away and doesn't do what he says?

We would never do that, would we?

- Put away "all filthiness and rampant wickedness" (1:21)—who would ignore that?
- "Visit orphans and widows in their affliction" (1:27)—don't we all do that?

- "Do not speak evil against one another, brothers" (4:11)—
  ever done that?

Do you see the point James is making? It is not easy, but it is so clear. When we listen *but do not do*, it is just like the woman who sees the greasy hair and the cereal on the cardigan and just carries on through the day regardless. To be spiritually whole, we must listen to God. And to be spiritually whole, we must not only listen. We must do.

We have seen already how profoundly influenced James is by the Jewish *Shema*. Luke Cheung notes that, "significantly, the Shema in Deuteronomy 6:4 begins with the call to *hear*, and then proceeds with the call to *act* in love."[2] The way of wholeness incorporates hearing and doing, like two sides of a coin. To have hearing only and not doing—to hear who God is and not respond with appropriate action—is utterly nonsensical for James. And in Deuteronomy 6:6–8 the immediate action that follows hearing is the call to place God's words in our hearts, then to teach them, then to talk about them, then to bind them to our bodies and to write them on the property we own. In other words, it is a call to the action of doing God's word.

We think that if we want to be whole, maybe God has to touch our hearts or change our hearts. Both are true, of course. But James is saying here in black and white that if you want to be whole, you also need to do what the Bible says. That is actually one of the ways God touches and changes our hearts.

The rest of this chapter will discuss what we must do.

Persevere with God's Freeing Law

"But the one who looks into the perfect law, the law of liberty, and perseveres, being no hearer who forgets but a doer who acts, he will be blessed in his doing" (James 1:25). Notice how James gives the

Bible another name at this point: "the perfect law, the law of liberty."
When you look in the Bible and listen to it, you're not just seeing
who you are, as in a mirror, but you're seeing who God is, coming
face-to-face with his character, his loves, his standards, his law. That
is what law does: it reveals the nature of the one who gives it.

"Don't play in the traffic" is an excellent law. It values life above
death for both pedestrians and commuters. It protects the life of
individuals and the well-being of communities. Every law that
God gives is like that: perfect. Do not murder; do not covet; do
not commit adultery; honor your mother and father; remember
the Sabbath day and keep it holy. These are moral imperatives that
reveal a perfect God, and a perfect life too, if only we could live it.

For this reason, James amplifies "perfect law" with this lovely
phrase: "the law of liberty" (1:25). Of course, nearly always we
think it's the opposite. Surely laws restrict freedom, hamper my
independence, stop me doing something? If a law is perfect, however, then the only way to be free is to live within it. That a fish
belongs in water might be a law of nature, but it is also a law of
liberty, for it sets the fish free to live in accordance with its nature.
So, when the parent opens the door to three-year-old Jack at seven
in the morning and says, "Off you go, run, be free: be all that you
were meant to be! Maybe we'll see you at dinner tonight," well, it
might look like freedom, but only of a perverse kind. No law is
given to the child in that situation, but this gift of freedom is, in
fact, abuse and neglect. Even the most radical libertarian would
agree that this is freeing Jack to experience harm.

When God speaks to us in his law and tells us how to live, what
to do and what not to do, these are commands given in accordance
with both our nature and his nature, and they are only ever given
for our flourishing. They are laws that set us free to be all that we

were meant to be as creatures in his world in relationship with him. The Book of Common Prayer beautifully describes God as the one "whose service is perfect freedom." It is why, in being the most obedient man who ever lived, the Lord Jesus was also the most free man who ever lived. In our human wisdom, however, we so often cut ourselves loose from the law of the Lord and ignore him. We love writing our own laws. Pretty quickly, we find that when we do this, we are not set free but in fact enslaved, held captive to whoever has the most power, the most money, the biggest army, or the most controlling government.

Now, it is one thing when the world cuts itself loose from God's law, and of course we see this all the time. Not long ago, a Dutchman sued his government to be allowed to change his age from sixty-nine to forty-nine. His argument was that we can change our names and our gender, so why couldn't he decide his own age? Well, it is one thing when people who don't know God refuse to look into the law of liberty, but that is not the tragedy in James's crosshairs here—it is when *God's people* stop persevering in looking into his law of liberty. We have the Bible; we love his word; we look in the mirror—and we ignore it. There are few greater tragedies in life than this, for acting on God's word by doing what it says is the only route to living in the power and blessing for which we have been created: "but a doer who acts, he will be blessed in his doing" (1:25). Doing the word makes you flourish. It will make you content. Whole. Righteous. The posture of the believer is to delight in the law of the Lord, both day and night (Ps. 1:2).[3]

So, the Bible is like a seed implanted inside you which can grow and give life. It is like a mirror that can tell you the truth about yourself and show you what you need to do. The Bible can set you free and give you the kind of life that is blessed by God.

Applying These Pictures of God's Word

I will now apply these pictures to our lives.

Remember, This Is Not a Word to the Overly Sensitive

It is worth saying that sometimes in my experience it is those who are most in Scripture who can have the most tender consciences. Some of us will read James 1:22 and think, "Well, I listen to sermons every week, and I don't always do what they say; or I try to but I fail, so am I just deceiving myself?"

We should remember that James is a letter to churches in perilous danger of behaving badly. It is written to church families who could soon be tearing themselves apart, precisely because they never miss a Sunday but they have absolutely no love in their hearts for the persons sitting next to them. The letter is written to proud Christians refusing to be humbled, refusing to "receive with meekness the implanted word" (1:21). Their Bibles are open, but their ears are shut, and they sure have a lot to say over coffee!

Here's another application to encourage us.

Learn How God Grows Us in Righteousness

I can well imagine you, as reader, saying to me: "Look, David, I've been at this for a long time and I'm still messing up. Here I am, still saying and doing things I shouldn't. I know James says, 'Therefore put away all filthiness and rampant wickedness and receive with meekness the implanted word, which is able to save your souls' (1:21). So, how do I actually do that? Please tell me!"

The little phrase "put away" is the same idea as taking something off. It's what you do when you come in from the rugby game, clobbered, and you're covered in mud and blood from head to toe. You take off the filthy uniform and put it away. James is using a clothing image. He is saying to stop wearing those things and get dressed instead with meekness; take off wickedness and put on humility. As you clothe yourself with what the Bible says, it will change you.

In *Beyond Personality* by C. S. Lewis there's a chapter called "Let's Pretend."[4] Originally broadcast for radio, it is one of my favorite pieces in all of his writings. He faces head-on how we might make sense of the Bible's language of taking off evil and putting away filthiness, and instead putting on good deeds such as compassion, patience, humility, and meekness. Come on, says Lewis, let's be honest; this is just playing let's pretend. For you might clothe yourself with compassion, but underneath you're still uncompassionate. You might put on meekness, but underneath you're as proud as ever before. And, says Lewis, who wants that kind of change? When all is said and done, if we are honest with ourselves and with God, we want to be different from the inside out, not putting these things on to cover up what we're really like. It is mere theater. It comes from the world of dressing up and make-believe. If anything, it accentuates, rather than heals, our split personalities.

Ah, yes, says Lewis, but don't forget there are two ways to pretend. There's a bad way to pretend and a good way. Someone might pretend to help you and reach out his hand, but as he does so, he's picking your pocket with the other one. For the con man, pretense obscures reality.

But the good way to pretend is when pretense leads to reality. Think about what small children are doing in so many of their games. They pretend to be grown-ups. They play moms and dads. Maybe you have seen this for yourself. The young girl walks across the living room in her mom's high heels, or she is wearing a doctor's uniform; the little boy is dressed as a firefighter or in a football jersey. Today the clothes are pretend, but one day they'll fit. Today they are just dressing up, but one day this might be what they'll wear every day. Lewis's point is that the child's pretense is not a made-up reality but an anticipatory reality in appropriate guise. It will one day give way to the reality. The wearing of what does not yet quite fit or really belong is part of growing up into adulthood, and into being the kind of person the child is meant to become.

If you want to be like the Lord Jesus Christ, from the inside out, then let both things happen. Dress yourself with meekness on the outside, and as you receive the word, the inside change will begin to happen too; and what you will find is that the inner growth catches up with the gospel clothes you're wearing on the outside. I find this a really beautiful idea and a tantalizing possibility to grasp. The gospel is not merely behavior change, surface deep, or window dressing but deep change, an implanted kind of change; so we need to learn how God grows that in us. He implants his truth and tells us to watch our speech, our actions, and our habits, and over time his word and the action together grow us in righteousness.

Let's get very practical in this next application. Here is something to do and to grow in, for which we will need the implanted word to help us.

Bridle Your Tongue

"Know this, my beloved brothers: let every person be quick to hear, slow to speak, slow to anger" (James 1:19). "If anyone thinks he is religious and does not bridle his tongue but deceives his heart, this person's religion is worthless" (1:26).

This is James giving it to us straight and shooting from the hip. The arrogant word, the malicious gossip, the naked hostility toward someone else expressed in words—well, when we speak like that, we are claiming knowledge of God while treating others in ways that give the lie to that claim. It is a particular mark of our sinfulness that we are able to claim knowledge of God yet go on to speak about people made in his image in ways which, were others to hear us, they would be perfectly justified in saying, "You don't really know God."[5] So, we measure our religion by our orthodoxy. We measure it according to which church we're in, what denomination we're part of, who our pastor is, or how we give our money, but James basically says, "Just let me listen to your words, and then I'll tell you how much your religion is actually worth." The inconsistency between our belief and our words is as crazy a way to live as looking in the mirror and doing nothing about the problems.

Roast preacher for lunch. Frozen congregation for dessert. A piece of gossip passed on as a prayer request. A tasty morsel that will wound and upset. An inability to forgive, presented as self-justification. When speech is destructive, calculated to benefit me and tear others down, then it says something about our receiving of God's word.

What do we text and why do we text it? How do we use email? James says it's the sent items that reveal religion. It's so challenging. Often, I've lain in bed at night and wondered why on earth I sent that email or text; I am not sure I've ever lain there and regretted *not* sending an email or a text. You'd think I would learn! I am still so quick to speak and so slow to listen. We think our religion is visible when we're in church, but in fact it lives in our DMs.[6] My tweets say so much more about my religion than the "About Me" page on our church website. If we don't see this, then we deceive our hearts (1:26).

Let me change the applications from personal to corporate now.

Remember That Our Church Structures Must Run Bibline

It used to be said about John Bunyan that if you were to cut him open, his blood would run bibline.[7] The living words of the living God were in his veins and coursing through his system. He had them implanted inside him. It was a way of saying that the Bible was so deeply in him that it poured out of him.

I have come to see that a useful way of evaluating all the structures of church life, everything from our buildings to our activities, is to imagine cutting them open and seeing if their lifeblood runs bibline. How vital are God's words to this particular structure? A principle of life in every domain is that structures tell stories. The way something is shaped to exist, or shaped to run, tells a story about the things we hold most dearly.

At Trinity Church here in Aberdeen, we have had the immense privilege, the great frustration, and the mind-numbing cost of recently working on a church renovation project (which I mentioned earlier). In working with an architect, I have learned that you can cut a building open and see a picture of it dissected from top to bottom. It can be opened so that you see all the floors on different levels at the same time.

As we did this on one occasion, looking at how the building might cohere as a hub for gospel ministry in our city, I wondered how our church family should work toward not ending up like the congregations James is writing to: speaking angry words, drawing ugly lines, and performing no good deeds. I looked at the vast array of physical spaces on offer and realized that the building we were about to renovate would grow our ministry and church family only if it ran bibline. Enter just about every room and the Bible must fall out of it. We have to implant the word of God into it and get the Bible coursing through its veins: the implanted word in our adult classes and children's Sunday school, in our youth groups and toddlers' groups, in our student suppers and over-sixties group. That will save us, and nothing else—it's not preparing the building for social action and mercy ministries that will do so.

I put it as starkly as that because I know from this passage just how important mercy ministries must be in an authentic gathering of Christ's people. "Religion that is pure and undefiled before God the Father is this: to visit orphans and widows in their affliction, and to keep oneself unstained from the world" (James 1:27). The Bible tells us we are to look after those who cannot look after themselves, and if we don't, we don't know God. As we planned to renovate our church premises, we were explicitly aware that we had to be like our heavenly Father by looking after those who cannot look after themselves.

But we also had to notice that James himself was showing us that social welfare comes from doing the Bible—not in competition with it, but rather with the Bible as the life source from which it flows. So, we need the Bible alive in our midst, and the Bible implanted within us, to let good deeds flow constantly from it, and out from us to those around us. Many a church and many a denomination go for social welfare and lose the Bible, and with no implanted word, the life of the body withers and dies on the vine. William Still, the much-loved minister of Gilcomston South Church in Aberdeen, used to say that the death of the church ministry lay in the birth of the church hall. More people readily come to activities than come to pray. Eventually, more gather to socialize than to worship.

What would James say? People gather to speak much more easily than they gather to listen, for we are quick to speak and slow to hear. We are slow to hear God, slow to listen to the Bible.

If you ever get the chance to be involved in designing or renovating a church building, let me encourage you in the simple task of starting with the pulpit and designing outward to every other part. If you are never in that position but you are actively involved in leading a church or running activities, ask whether the Bible's absence from the event would make any difference to the lifeblood of why and how it functions. If its absence would allow that ministry to carry on unaffected, then you are cutting it open and finding that the lifeblood is something other than bibline.

Examine Where You Are with the Bible

Close the book now and take some time out for some honest reflection on where you are with the Bible. Is your love for the Scriptures deepening year after year in your walk with the Lord Jesus, or is the word feeling less implanted and more uprooted?

It could be that the way to approach this question is to ask where you are with the Lord Jesus himself. R. C. Sproul said, "There is an inseparable relationship between your affection for Christ and your affection for the Scriptures."[8] If your relationship with the Bible has cooled, it is likely that a cooling relationship with Jesus has followed hand in hand, and vice versa.

The reason for taking time to reflect like this is that I know from personal experience how very easy it is to watch other people looking in a mirror and to see what they need to change, and to worry more about them than about myself. It's like parents with teenagers. We can see what they should see about their hair, their clothes, or their shoes, and yet off they go, oblivious. They couldn't care less—but surely everyone can see they're a mess! We notice other people's blind spots so much more quickly than our own. My weekly location as a preacher behind a pulpit, looking at all sorts of people who have so much to change, reminds me of this all the time. There is so much to change in the church, and so rarely do I think that it begins with me!

So, where are you with Christ and his word? Do you nod at its truth? Do you expect the Bible to comfort but never rebuke you? To encourage you and exhort you but never to humble or admonish you? When was the last time a behavior changed, an action started or stopped, because of what the Bible says?

There are few marks for hearing or listening in God's kingdom. But *doing* is what draws the praise of Jesus and causes us to hear his voice: "Well done, good and faithful servant" (Matt. 25:23). It is the same voice that says to us,

> But this is the one to whom I will look:
>   he who is humble and contrite in spirit
>   and trembles at my word. (Isa. 66:2)

Questions for Discussion or Personal Reflection

1. As you look in the mirror now, what does your own input/output evaluation reveal?

2. Are there specific types of words that you want to stop speaking?

3. How does C. S. Lewis's idea of "pretending" help you see the connection between heart change and what we do?

4. What are the specific things that you can begin to put on or put away in the week ahead?

5. Where are you with the Lord Jesus and his word? Take time to reflect now.

3

Love

*The goal is not to have weaker desires but stronger desires
. . . to have righteous desires surpass evil desires. . . .
The desire to love and follow Christ must be a sweeter
song to us than the music of the world and our flesh.*

A. CRAIG TROXEL, *WITH ALL YOUR HEART*

[26] If anyone thinks he is religious and does not bridle his tongue but deceives his heart, this person's religion is worthless. [27] Religion that is pure and undefiled before God the Father is this: to visit orphans and widows in their affliction, and to keep oneself unstained from the world.

[1] My brothers, show no partiality as you hold the faith in our Lord Jesus Christ, the Lord of glory. [2] For if a man wearing a gold ring and fine clothing comes into your assembly, and a poor man in shabby clothing also comes in, [3] and if you pay attention to the one who wears the fine clothing and say, "You sit here in a good place," while you say to the poor man, "You stand over there," or, "Sit down at my feet," [4] have you not then made distinctions among yourselves and become judges with evil thoughts? [5] Listen, my beloved brothers, has not God chosen those who are poor in the world to be rich in faith and heirs of the kingdom, which he

has promised to those who love him? ⁶ But you have dishonored the poor man. Are not the rich the ones who oppress you, and the ones who drag you into court? ⁷ Are they not the ones who blaspheme the honorable name by which you were called?

⁸ If you really fulfill the royal law according to the Scripture, "You shall love your neighbor as yourself," you are doing well. ⁹ But if you show partiality, you are committing sin and are convicted by the law as transgressors. ¹⁰ For whoever keeps the whole law but fails in one point has become guilty of all of it. ¹¹ For he who said, "Do not commit adultery," also said, "Do not murder." If you do not commit adultery but do murder, you have become a transgressor of the law. ¹² So speak and so act as those who are to be judged under the law of liberty. ¹³ For judgment is without mercy to one who has shown no mercy. Mercy triumphs over judgment.

JAMES 1:26–2:13

WHAT DO YOU LOVE?

What kinds of things do you love?

Whom do you love?

There are going to be all kinds of answers to these questions. I love my dog; I love my kids; I love my friends; I love skiing; I love to sleep in; I love making it to the top of a mountain. These things, and countless others besides, are good and beautiful and worthy of our affections.

In this chapter, I want to let James tell us something surprising about our loves. James knows what you love, and he knows whom you love. So far, I've used medical terms to help us understand this epistle: James is like the most skillful of doctors, with the ability to diagnose heart disease. So, as we sit with James again in his surgery, his diagnosis continues, and here's what he says to us: "I can see what you love—you love glory."

Do you know that about yourself? I hope you do. Consider all your other loves that you thought of just a moment ago: you love them because there is something glorious about them. The view from the top of the mountain. Your loved one's face. God has made us glory-hungry creatures; we're drawn to it.

Recall where God put Adam and Eve. He placed them in a garden where there was a river that flowed to water the earth, where there were food and beauty and delight in abundance. Many scholars have come to see that Eden was the first tabernacle and temple, the first place in the cosmos where heaven and earth kissed, and where God and humanity dwelt together in perfect harmony. It was a place of glory.[1] James's basic assumption, as he writes this part of his letter, is that we are wired to love glory. In everyday life, we speak, act, think, and make decisions in hundreds of ways that reflect our hearts' attraction to glory. We are glory chasers.

For several years, each Monday evening I got to watch about fifteen young boys chase glory. Mile End Primary School football team probably hasn't made it into your fantasy football league. Yet. But the love of glory is there for all to see. A goal is scored and a ten-year-old boy feels like he has won the World Cup. He pumps his fists, arms outstretched, and the adulation flows: oh, the glory! Each week we would give the Player of the Week trophy to take home, and let me assure you, that little piece of molded plastic shone all night long in glory beside a young boy's bed. On more than one occasion I am sure it was even cradled all night long.

We love glory. It is all around us in so many beautiful ways. On the morning when I first preached this passage in our church, we had the baptism of a child of Christian parents. Baptizing is one of the most wonderful things I get to do. You may have read Marilynne Robinson's exquisite novel *Gilead*. At one point, John Ames reflects on what it's like to have children in your life as he watches his son shimmer in spray of the garden sprinkler, and he speaks about the glory of baptizing a baby: "That feeling of a baby's brow against the palm of your hand—how I have loved this life."[2] You don't need to share my theology of baptism to agree that few things in life, or in the Bible itself, generate as much wonder and awe as new life within a home and within the covenant people of God.

You can replace this example with any number of things in your own life. From babies to buildings, from places to possessions, we love things that are beautiful. In this section, James takes the layers off this love to show us that this is a love of glory that says both something wonderful about us and something truly terrible about us. Our good love of glory has become twisted and corrupted, and our greatest glories show what kind of heart we have. Like James's first readers, we are shown to have heart disease.

So, the surgeon's knife is in James's hand. It is possible to love a kind of glory that shows that we have "become judges with evil thoughts" (2:4). Do you ever think of yourself as evil because of what you love? Now, this is hard to hear. But taking it in and pondering it deeply is important, for it might save your soul.

We will see James explain how the aim of a single heart, purely devoted to God, is not compromised by loving others as well. Here is Richard Bauckham's summary of what we will explore:

Wholeness occurs when the whole of human life is focused and integrated in God. It receives from God the complete law and complete wisdom, adequate to encompass the whole of life. It responds to God in wholehearted faith (1:5–8), in wholehearted love (1:12; 2:5) and in fulfilling the complete law (1:22–25; 2:8–11). The last is summed up in the commandment to love one's neighbour as oneself (2:8), an all-inclusive and non-discriminating love of one's fellows. This is not, in the end, an addition to the love of God, as though it provided an alternative point of focus and integration of life. Rather, love of God entails love of neighbour. One cannot love God without loving the neighbour.[3]

We will look at how we can emulate God, under two headings about loving and judging.

Learn to Love as God Loves

"My brothers, show no partiality as you hold the faith in our Lord Jesus Christ, the Lord of glory" (James 2:1). This command about not treating people unequally is, in fact, the basis for what is about to become a blistering indictment of our twisted love of glory. "For if a man wearing a gold ring and fine clothing comes into your assembly, and a poor man in shabby clothing also comes in . . ." (2:2).

The glory is there in the gold ring, the luxury branded suit, the House of Whatever label that would make you sit up and take notice. There is a very specific problem here: it seems the rich were harming and oppressing this church family, and in the culture of the time the division between rich and poor was really obvious in how folks dressed. That may or may not be as obvious in our culture today, but James's words to us are still so challenging. Whether it's dress code or zip code, the car you drive or the school your children attend, this is a passage about "partiality" (2:1, 9) and about making "distinctions among yourselves" (2:4).

Today we would call it favoritism. We are drawn to people we like. Magnetically, we move toward people who can give us things and do things for us, and in whose glory we can bask. To the people who look and smell and sound good, and who do great things, we want to say, in effect, "You sit here in a good place" (2:3). It happens all the time in churches throughout the land, and I'm sure it has happened in the one I attend too. But to the "poor man in shabby clothing" (2:2) we say, "You stand over there," or, "Sit down at my feet" (2:3), as if to say, "You have no glory worthy of my time and attention and effort." If we're really honest, this is how we love. We love

- human wealth (money and resources and comfort),
- human intelligence (degrees and PhDs and stimulating conversation), and
- human strength (sport and youth and skill).

We are so partial to all those things. We love their glory.

I once had coffee with someone who was fabulously wealthy, the kind of wealth to make your eyes water. I sat with him and talked with him, and let me tell you, I didn't want to leave him. I found myself profoundly allured by the world he inhabits. Maybe it's just me. But it comes so naturally to all of us, I suspect. We bask in it, and it kind of rubs off on us so that we want some of it too. This person has resources from which the gospel work I'm involved in could really benefit. Why, yes, sure, of course I've got time for a second cup of coffee! My two o'clock appointment? Oh, don't worry; that person can wait. Leaving this plush place in a hurry? Not a chance! I'm all yours.

And James comes up beside me as I sit there, puts the stethoscope on my heart, and just listens. Ah, yes, I can hear what you love. The stethoscope is telling me how in your heart you divide people up into significant, skilled, useful, and attractive and not so significant, less useful—and look, here it is, that divided heart spilling right out into the open, with you separating people in the way you treat them.

"Right," says James, as he takes off his stethoscope; "that's how *you* love. You love this kind of glory. Now let me tell you how *God* loves." Did you spot that in our passage? "Religion that is pure and undefiled before God the Father is this: to visit orphans and widows in their affliction, and to keep oneself unstained from the world" (1:27). This verse comes immediately before 2:1, and this is one of those very many instances in the Bible where chapter divisions are most unhelpful to the flow of argument and thought. James is saying what God likes to see in church (1:27), and then goes straight into what a sick church likes to see in church (2:1), and when we read it through in one go, the contrast could not be more shocking.

We are told to love and care for orphans and widows (1:27), and so the implication is that we should love and care for the man in shabby clothing no less than for the person in fine clothes. We are told to do this because it's the kind of religion that pleases God *the Father*. God loves as Father. As a perfect Father. Pity the home where the father's love shows partiality. Favoritism. We all joke about the fair-haired boy, but how awful if such a thing is actually true in a family. Good fathers who love well don't discriminate. They don't say to the eldest daughter, "You sit here in a good place," and to the youngest daughter, "You stand over there at the back or sit at my feet." And God is our perfect heavenly Father, so we should love like he does.

Orphans and widows. This is not, of course, a definitive list, as if choosing to visit only these groups makes our religion pure and undefiled. Rather, they are representative examples of the kinds of people who are unable to look after themselves. That's who God loves. But do you? Do I? Such people are unrewarding. James is probing deeply to enquire if we know that God loves his world in the same way as a father loves his children. A good dad loves his weak, defenseless children. In the same way, God the Father loves those who have nothing in the tank to give him back, who have no human glory to be proud of, who shrink down low in his presence and cannot lift up their heads for shame. He loves the person in shabby clothes. Look how God loves, and compare it to how we love.

I need to ask myself again, "When was the last time someone utterly unrewarding in every way received my love?" And by that I mean actual love, real time, real attention, and real care.

Maybe, already, God is speaking to you while you read these lines. This is such a challenge. It is a call to examine what our inner, divided heart loves look like when they come out into the open.

But James isn't finished with us yet.

"Listen, my beloved brothers, has not God chosen those who are poor in the world to be rich in faith and heirs of the kingdom, which he has promised to those who love him?" (2:5). If you want to see how God loves, look whom he chooses. That's what James is saying. Think about it: no one chooses the poor; we choose the rich, the glory.

At the end of each training session with my Mile End boys we played a football match, the part of the evening they always relished. If I had left them to choose the teams, though, there would have been glory-battle bloodshed—total carnage. We would have had the strong players, probably all good friends with each other, battering the weaker players 30–0. And I can guarantee that all the winning team would have gone home and slept soundly in their beds without a care in the world, bathed in glory. It was actually an act of love on my part, as their coach, to choose the weak, to put them on a good team, to make an overlooked player the captain for the night. That's love, isn't it?

Do you realize God has done that with you? "Oh, I'm so insignificant, David. No one knows me. I contribute nothing. I'm not rich, and my home circumstances mean I can't give to the building project or the church funds, and I'm kind of ashamed about it. I'm overlooked, marginalized, ignored." But James says that God chose you! He chose you to be on his team. Please read 2:5 again, climb up inside it, and let its light wash over you.

God takes the weak and the poor, and he loves them—that's glorious. But instead, we ignore that. We take the strong and the rich and we love them. "No," says James. "Keep doing that and you will destroy your church. You'll ruin it."

Maybe, as you have read the passage, you've spotted how James has set us up with two different types of glory: "My brothers, show no partiality as you hold the faith in our Lord Jesus Christ, the Lord of glory" (2:1).

Here's how this passage works: you confess the faith, you're true believers in our Lord Jesus Christ, and so you say you're following the Lord of glory, but you act like you believe in glorious people. Look how that flows in the argument. As you hold the faith in the Lord Jesus, the Lord of glory, show no partiality, "For if a man wearing a gold ring and fine clothing comes into your assembly . . ." (2:1–2). You say you believe in Jesus's glory, but it is clear that your heads are so easily turned by human glory. You are looking at Jesus, but in comes the money man, and, see, you drop your gaze and turn your head, and as you do so, you show the kind of glory your heart really loves.

I love the phrase "our Lord Jesus Christ, the Lord of glory" (2:1). It means that in our world there is one person of absolute beauty and truth and goodness. There is someone who is just pure goodness all the way through: no shadow, no dark side, no secret vices, no selfishness that comes out now and then. He only speaks truth; he only loves what is right; he never serves himself. In the Lord Jesus, God has given us someone who is absolute beauty, truth, and goodness all the way through. He walked this earth untainted, unbroken, and unspoiled, and glory shines from every part of his life, words, death, and resurrection. Jesus Christ is indeed the Lord of glory.

Note how this title for the Lord Jesus (2:1) immediately follows the reference to pure and undefiled religion as that which cares for "orphans and widows in their affliction" (1:27). These are the two key categories for the oppressed and the defenseless in the Old Testament, and it is highly significant that again and again God introduces himself as "Father of the fatherless and protector of widows" (Ps. 68:5; see also Deut. 10:17–18; Ps. 146:7–9). Tim Keller quotes Vinoth Ramachandra in saying that this is "scandalous justice." Whereas in other ancient cultures the power of their gods was directed to, and through, the social elites and the movers and shakers in society, the God of the Bible, in stark contrast, stands out "from the gods of all other religions as a God on the side of the powerless, and of justice for the poor."[4]

That James should apply the title "Lord of glory" to Jesus so soon after this description of the kind of religion that honors God is no coincidence. James is saying that the glory of God is seen in the Lord Jesus, who showed no partiality—he did not make divisions between those who were worthy of him and those who were not. We remember how Jesus regarded children when even his disciples wanted to push them away (Matt. 19:13–15), and his compassion for the widow who had lost her only son (Luke 7:11–17). We recall how he summoned tax collectors (Matt. 9:9–13), and how he responded to a woman caught in sin (John 8:1–11), and to a woman who risked everything by engaging in displays of broken-hearted, repentant affection for him (Luke 7:36–50). This Jesus, the Lord of glory, welcomed all to his side. If *he* did so, who are we to do otherwise?

So, allow James to ask you: "Can you see the Lord Jesus clearly? Can you see his glory? His greatness and his goodness?" I imagine that the very reason why you are reading this book in the first place is that you do have sight of who Jesus is, and you love him. Now James is effectively asking: "Do you love *like* him? Do you hold to faith in our Lord Jesus Christ, the Lord of glory, but it's just that: a belief?" It doesn't drive your actions. In short, you *believe* in the Lord of glory, but you *love* human glory.

The message of this part of this wonderful epistle is that only a clear sight of who the Lord Jesus is will let you see other people clearly. Unless I am dazzled by Christ's glory, I will be amazed at your glory if you come to me with success and money and prestige and lots of ways to benefit me. I will choose you to be on my team. Conversely, unless I'm dazzled by Christ's glory, I'll be disappointed in your lack of glory and let down by what you can't give me.

In the last chapter of this book, the application was essentially this: What am I speaking? In this chapter it's even deeper: To whom am I speaking? Do I love my brothers and sisters in my head only, or in my actions or in my words too? The people to whom you speak reveal the Lord you love, and the people we prioritize display the glory we prize.

Whom do you choose to speak to at church? Whom do you gravitate toward at coffee time? Seating choices can reveal glory horizons too. You will not love those you find unrewarding unless Jesus is glorious to you, and if you're looking for glory on earth, then you will love glorious people.

As challenging as all of this is, James wants to bring it home to us even more. Just as we get up to leave his surgery, he says, "Oh, just one more thing before you go."

Learn to Judge as God Judges

"If you really fulfill the royal law according to the Scripture, 'You shall love your neighbor as yourself,' you are doing well" (James 2:8). At first, this seems quite a gear change, but it is actually still all about partiality. If you show partiality between people, then you are showing it toward God's law, and that is a very dangerous place to be. "But if you show partiality, you are committing sin and are convicted by the law as transgressors. For whoever keeps the whole law but fails in one point has become guilty of all of it" (2:9–10). We think of ourselves as merely partial lawbreakers. We've broken that law over there but kept most of the rest. James says that's not how the law works: it comes as a unity. We treat the Ten Commandments like a ten-question test. Break four of them, we think, and our score is six out of ten. Maybe the next day we have a seven-out-of-ten kind of day. In fact, says James, break just one of the commandments and the whole law lies broken at your feet.

Some time ago, I was on a very long train journey on a very long train. In the car where I was sitting there were five windows along each side: ten in total. If I had taken the emergency hammer down from the ceiling and, with the train en route to its next stop, had casually smashed two windows within reach of my seat, how much of the train would I have damaged? I might have broken only two windows, but I would have marred the whole train for everyone on board. The journey would have been over, and my relationship with the people responsible for the entire train, seriously impaired. It wouldn't have got me very far to point out how many windows I had thoughtfully left untouched by the hammer's tender mercies.

James wants us to understand that if we break one of the commandments, then we have damaged our whole relationship with God. "For he who said, 'Do not commit adultery,' also said, 'Do not murder.' If you do not commit adultery but do murder, you have become a transgressor of the law" (2:11). Notice something very telling. We divide the law up into different sections: discrete laws, a bit here which we find rather hard to obey, a bit there which is easier. We divide the very thing that God himself simply calls "the law" (2:11). It's what we do, and doing so reflects who we are. But the one God regards his law as one. It is whole. The fracture is on our side, not his.

If you don't love the poor man, the unrewarding man, you have broken the whole law. No point saying: "Well, yes, I ignored him and couldn't care less about him. But I didn't murder him and I didn't sleep with his wife. They're the big commands, aren't they? I'm sure God's cool with that; he'll understand." Show favoritism, and the law convicts you as a transgressor. No love, then you are guilty.

This passage is all about judgment and how we judge compared with how God judges. "Have you not then made distinctions among yourselves and become judges with evil thoughts?" (2:4). If we show partiality, one to another over another, we've used our broken law keeping, our non-love of our neighbor, as our criterion for judging, and that's just plain evil. It leaves God's law broken on the floor while we decide which people to love.

And yet, here's what we've forgotten: while we judge, we too will one day be judged ourselves. "So speak and so act as those who are to be judged under the law of liberty" (2:12). We might have neglected the perfect law of liberty in our judging, but God won't neglect it when it's his turn.

James is putting this kind of imaginary scenario in front of us: You're at the church door one day, and a rich man and a poor man come in. Which one will you speak to, and why? Then, says James, imagine this: Now it's your turn to be walking into God's assembly, into his presence in heaven at the end of your life. It's no longer *you* at the door, looking at rich and poor coming in and determining status based on who most catches your eye. Now *God* is the one at the door, and you're coming into *his* house. In you go, holding in your hands the two broken tablets of stone, the Ten Commandments. You're frantically trying to put them back together because you broke them. You smashed the whole law into bits by not loving your neighbor as yourself, yet now you find yourself in God's presence and desperately trying to unite what you pulled apart.

You stand before God the Judge. What do you need?

Just one thing: mercy.

You have trashed his royal law and trampled his kingdom standards, and so the only thing you can do is beg for mercy. If we're honest, over time many Christians think that showing mercy is kind of what God is there for: of course, he'll treat me favorably. But James says: "For judgment is without mercy to one who has shown no mercy. Mercy triumphs over judgment" (2:13).

We want mercy from God? Then we need to ask ourselves, how much mercy did we show the person who needed mercy from us?

The poor man. The person with nothing to give us. Did we give him something: attention, time, care, love—mercy? If we didn't, then why do we want it for ourselves from God? Who do we think we are?

Here is a very challenging piece of James's gospel medicine: only a clear sight of how God judges will enable us to judge other people rightly. We judge with glory spectacles on: he looks nice; she can give me good things. But God judges based on his mercy.

I suspect there might well be someone in your life toward whom it would be very hard to show mercy if he or she were to turn up at your door. Maybe it would be almost impossible for you.

"Well," says Dr. James. "I get that. But what will you want from God when you turn up at his door?"

"Oh, some justice, God. Yes, please. Just what I came here for. Glad I came!"

No, I don't think that's what we'll ask for at the end. I know this for myself: without mercy, I'm done for; I'm finished.

James is crystal clear and so lovingly direct as he speaks to us: dear friends, brothers, and sisters, change how you speak and change how you act. Let's do it now. Let's change it together. Today.

Questions for Discussion or Personal Reflection

1. Can you see any concrete ways in your own life in which your belief in the "Lord of glory" is dominated by your heart's love of human glory?

2. Can you think of any things that would be different in your church family if there were no favoritism at all of any kind?

3. "The people we prioritize display the glory we prize." Reflect on the key people in your life and in your church. Is there anything you need to change personally in relation to them?

4. In what ways does God judge? How could a love of mercy change your relationships with God and with others around you?

5. At this point in the book, what are you praying for and asking God to change in you?

4

Seeing

Grace cannot be severed from its fruits. If God gives you
St Paul's faith, you will soon have St James' works.

AUGUSTUS TOPLADY, *THE WORKS OF AUGUSTUS M. TOPLADY*

[14] What good is it, my brothers, if someone says he has faith but does not have works? Can that faith save him? [15] If a brother or sister is poorly clothed and lacking in daily food, [16] and one of you says to them, "Go in peace, be warmed and filled," without giving them the things needed for the body, what good is that? [17] So also faith by itself, if it does not have works, is dead.

[18] But someone will say, "You have faith and I have works." Show me your faith apart from your works, and I will show you my faith by my works. [19] You believe that God is one; you do well. Even the demons believe—and shudder! [20] Do you want to be shown, you foolish person, that faith apart from works is useless? [21] Was not Abraham our father justified by works when he offered up his son Isaac on the altar? [22] You see that faith was active along with his works, and faith was completed by his works; [23] and the Scripture was fulfilled that says, "Abraham believed God, and it was counted to him as righteousness"—and he was called a friend of God. [24] You see that a person is justified by works and

not by faith alone. [25] And in the same way was not also Rahab the prostitute justified by works when she received the messengers and sent them out by another way? [26] For as the body apart from the spirit is dead, so also faith apart from works is dead.

JAMES 2:14–26

DID YOU KNOW that you can see faith? Actually see it with your own eyes?

In churches that prioritize the Bible, teaching faith in the Lord Jesus as the only way to be right with God, it is very easy to think of faith as being like a gas, such as oxygen. We know it's there, and it's real, but it's invisible. Faith is a belief; it's a brain thing. It's merely internal, personal and private.

In chapter 2, James wants to leave us in no doubt that this is false. In fact, it is a pernicious lie. You can actually see faith. With the eyes in your head, you can literally see it!

So often we want to know what following Christ means in all the nitty-gritty. We want our preachers and our small group Bible studies to spell out for us what it looks like to be a Christian in every corner of our lives. James is willing to lay the practical Christianity on thick for us, just as we asked, but this is likely to make things more difficult for us in the short run. For he just keeps smacking us between the eyes with direct, hard-hitting, bold, punchy applications to our lives, and here is what he is going to tell us in this chapter: if you can't see your faith, maybe that's because it's not there. It's not real. Ouch!

In Mark's Gospel, a paralyzed man is lowered to Jesus through the roof of a house. Dried mud and sticks and clay fall to the ground in a shower of dust (Mark 2:1–12). It is an amazing story. A group of friends have taken a man they love and care for, and because they can't get him to Jesus through the door, they get him to Jesus through the roof. They carry, climb, and dig, and they lower the man into the room suspended on ropes. Mark writes, "And when Jesus saw their faith . . ." (2:5). There it is: Jesus *saw* their faith. It led them to do something.

Maybe James was there in the crowd, for he was Jesus's half-brother, after all. Maybe he saw this himself. I think that as James reflected on an incident like that from the ministry of Jesus, he would say that the faith of those friends was alive, not dead. That's James's way of describing that story. Real faith is living faith, active faith.

By the time you finish this chapter, I want you to know that faith grows hands and feet. Faith climbs stairs, ties ropes, bends knees. Faith sweats, sends emails, cooks meals, plants churches, builds hospitals, flies to the other side of the world, and spends itself in servant form. That's what saving faith in the Lord Jesus means.

Let me ask at the outset: Just how practical do you want the gospel to be?

I will give us two warnings to heed, one problem to wrestle with, and then three applications to live out.

Warning 1: Don't Be All Talk and No Action

"What good is it, my brothers, if someone says he has faith but does not have works? Can that faith save him?" (James 2:14). This one verse asks two rhetorical questions. Faith that does not come with good works stapled to it, as an integral part of that faith, does not save. What good is it? None. Can that faith save? No. As we walk through these verses, it is vital to note the details and not rush too quickly. As Robert Plummer points out, James does not say that this imaginary person actually has faith, not works; rather, the person "says" he has faith. James's implicit view is that what the person says is actually false.[1] This is strengthened by the word "that," which appears before the word "faith" at the end of the verse. *That* type of faith is a self-declared but ultimately false kind.

"If a brother or sister is poorly clothed and lacking in daily food, and one of you says to them, 'Go in peace, be warmed and filled,' without giving them the things needed for the body, what good is that?" (2:15–16). Have you ever said to someone, "Let me know if I can help," in the knowledge that you expect the mere phrase itself to do some heavy lifting? I have. Of course, it's not that the phrase itself is always wrong. But wouldn't it be better, usually, just to help? Speech like this is our way of using our mouths to recognize a need but not using our resources to solve it. We somehow think, like this person in verse 16, that if we pronounce a kind of verbal blessing on someone, it will cover our real indifference to his or her plight. I find it so easy to say, "I'm praying for you," and so much harder actually to stop and pray. But, James is saying, such talk is cheap. All we've done is wagged our tongues in the direction of others.[2]

So, a talking faith only is dead faith.

Warning 2: Don't Be All Thought and No Action

This second point is very like the first one, but with a slight difference. Dead faith doesn't just show itself in our words; it can be in our minds, too.

"But someone will say, 'You have faith and I have works.' Show me your faith apart from your works, and I will show you my faith by my works" (James 2:18). Imagine the type of person who says: "Now, now, James, there are just different types of Christians out

98

there. Spirit Christians and word Christians. There are the doctrinal, theological types, and then there are the practical, doing types. There are faith Christians and there are doing Christians, works Christians. I say tomāto; you say tomäto. Right, James? We're all different."

Straight away, James shuts this down. Again, we should be careful with the details. James is crystal clear that this is not a case of faith *plus* works, as if genuine faith exists without works. Plummer explains: "James does not say that works need to be added to faith in order for one to be saved. Instead, his explicit language is that faith either 'has' or 'does not have' works (v. 17)."[3] James is saying that you cannot show me your faith separated off from works, because if you try to pull apart faith and works, all you have left are theological statements. "You believe that God is one; you do well. Even the demons believe—and shudder!" (2:19). It is a great truth that there is one true and living God, but if we say that's what living faith is, simply believing that truth, well, look who else believes it—the demons. They've got the same faith as you, and here's the point: it doesn't make them Christians! It doesn't save them. And, in fact, they believe and actually do something with that truth: they "shudder." What a word! The truth sends a shiver down their spines; they know God is real, and they are terrified.

At this point, several things in James are coming together. Notice how he is joining together at the deepest possible level two things we can tend to divorce (faith and works), and explicitly in a place where the *Shema* of Deuteronomy 6 is once again in view as the great confession of the faith. Only, here, belief in the oneness of God is something that is shared with demonic beings, so that the point is that mere knowledge, merely hearing, that the Lord is one is not enough to evidence genuine faith unless followed by the whole *Shema*, which includes a response of loving obedience with our whole beings. It is a brilliant piece of argumentation. Faith and works can no more be divorced in the life of the Christian than hearing and then loving the one true God can be divorced.

You've finished your courses and got your degrees, you've answered every theological question correctly, and you are oh so orthodox and oh so knowledgeable, *and it is not enough to show that you have faith that counts for anything.* For theology doesn't save; information doesn't save. What saves is faith in Jesus Christ that you can actually see in love, obedience, faithfulness, and joy—faith in action. As one writer has well said, "It is a good thing to possess an accurate theology, but it is unsatisfactory unless that good theology also possesses us."[4]

So, don't be all mouth and no action; don't be all thought and no action.

And yet, isn't there a problem?

A Problem to Wrestle With

"You see that a person is justified by works and not by faith alone" (James 2:24).

The problem is clear: Does James understand the gospel? Aren't we saved precisely by faith alone? Hasn't James ever heard of the apostle Paul?

Keep James 2:24 in your mind as you hear Paul's words: "For we hold that one is justified by faith apart from works of the law" (Rom. 3:28). This is why we believe in justification by faith *alone.* The apostle Paul and, in fact, the whole Bible are clear that the only way to be saved is by faith alone in Christ alone. It is a beautiful truth which lay at the heart of the Protestant Reformation, and which God's people have treasured from the dawn of time. James picks up the incredible story of Abraham offering his son Isaac on the altar in Genesis 22, but we know from Genesis 15 and 17 that

Abraham had saving faith in God before he did anything else, even before he was circumcised.

The glory of faith alone in Christ alone is treasured in song most Sundays in our churches. We love to sing words like this:

> No separation from the world,
> No work I do, no gift I give,
> Can cleanse my conscience, cleanse my hands;
> I cannot cause my soul to live.
> But Jesus died and rose again—
> The pow'r of death is overthrown!
> My God is merciful to me
> And merciful in Christ alone.[5]

Yet James says, "You see that a person is justified by works and not by faith alone" (2:24). So, what do we do with this?

Many people have stumbled here, of course. Surely James is wrong and Paul is right, or maybe Paul is wrong and James is right, they reason. This is why the great Martin Luther felt the epistle of James didn't really belong in our Bible—James seems to undermine the great cause of Reformation faith.

But there is a better way of reading James here. There are other parts of the Bible that seem to contradict each other, and sometimes it's not just different authors but what appear to be glaring contradictions within the same book, or even the same chapter, as here:

> Answer not a fool according to his folly,
>   lest you be like him yourself.
> Answer a fool according to his folly,
>   lest he be wise in his own eyes. (Prov. 26:4–5)

Should we, or shouldn't we, answer a fool according to his folly? The answer, of course, is both. It all depends on the type of twit in front of you. Some fools shouldn't be given the time of day. Others, well, there is real wisdom in taking the time to play their folly out in front of them. You have to work out which type of person you've got in front of you. To do that, context is king.

I think it's exactly like that with Paul and James. Often in the most polemical parts of his writings the apostle Paul has in his sights the kind of person who believes works are necessary to get eternal life. The person needs to have faith, yes, but that faith is not enough. It needs a top-up. Circumcision for a start, but then the food laws. Plant a church or two. Be a missionary. Attend church all your life, and then you'll make it in.

To this kind of confusion, Paul always has a very simple response: "No. It's wrong." Often Paul uses Abraham to win his argument, because it's clear that Abraham was justified *before* he was circumcised. The chronology matters. He had faith before his works came to light, which means that faith alone saves.

But James has a different type of problem, and a different type of person, in front of him. James wants a word with the person who says: "Because I have faith, I can put my feet up. I assent with my mouth and I believe with my mind, so the rest of my body is irrelevant. Faith in Jesus? Yes, got it. And now I can live as I please. Such faith in Christ does not have to make any difference whatsoever to my life. Such faith is my 'go-to-heaven-when-I-die' ticket, and now I can get on with the rest of my life my way."

To this kind of confusion, James has a very simple response: "No. It's wrong." The great glorious doctrine of justification by faith alone is true, and the faith that justifies is not alone. James's focus is not on *how* a person is justified before God; his point is how we can *see* that they are justified. For James, you see that someone is justified only when you see that saving faith alive and kicking.

This means that Abraham functions differently, in an illustrative way, for James than he does for Paul. Chris Bruno explains: "James is standing in Genesis 22, *looking back* at Abraham's faith in God's covenant promises that was confirmed by his ongoing obedience. However, Paul is focused on Abraham's initial belief in Genesis 12 and 15, *looking forward* to Abraham's works of faith."[6] As R. Kent Hughes puts it: "Paul says works cannot bring us to Christ. James says after we come to Christ they are imperative."[7]

James makes his point explicitly in 2:24 with his first two words: "You see." At first, you probably read those words the way I say them all the time: "You see, here's what I mean," or, "You see, here's the point." But James doesn't mean them like that. He intends no comma after "You see." He means it literally. You see that you are holding a book in your hands. You see that you are seated on a chair. You see that a person is justified. How? By what that person says or thinks? No, by what he or she *does*.

James is essentially saying to these Christians: "You belong to Jesus Christ. You're justified by faith. Yes, I can see that you're his because, look, you're like him. You love your neighbor as yourself. You care for the brothers and sisters. I can see what you've done with your money, your time, your food."

Several years ago, the Olympic gold-medal-winning archer Darrell Pace gave an archery exhibition in New York City's Central Park. All the major news stations were there. Shooting steel-tipped hunting arrows, Pace punctured bull's-eyes one after the other without a miss. Then he called for a volunteer.

"All you have to do," said Pace, "is hold this apple in your hand, waist-high." ABC correspondent Josh Howell stepped boldly forward. He stood there, a small apple in his hand, a large lump in his throat. Pace took aim from thirty yards away while a watching world held its breath. An arrow zipped through the air. He scored a clean hit that exploded the apple before striking the target behind. It was an astonishing sight.

(A funny aside was that, as soon as it was over, Howell's cameraman stepped forward really sheepishly and said he'd had a problem with his viewfinder and "didn't get it," so could he do it all again?)[8]

Here's the question: Can you see Josh Howell's faith? How many people in the crowd believed Darrell Pace could hit the apple? Probably several. But how much of their faith could you see? Only one person stepped forward and put his money where his mouth was. You could only see one man's faith. He didn't just believe it, or say that he did. He got up, took action, and lived out in a death-defying way his trust in Darrell Pace.

If you can't see your faith, maybe that's because it's not real. If you can't see it, and I can't see it, and others can't see it, is it actually there?

Three Applications to Reflect On

A Word to Every Reader

James 2:14–26 is all about an unbreakable union—faith and works—and what God has joined together let no church put asunder. So, are you divorcing what God has married?

"For as the body apart from the spirit is dead, so also faith apart from works is dead" (2:26). Divorce body and spirit, and you have a corpse on your hands. Separate them from each other, and life is over. Bodies lie motionless when there is no spirit, no soul, no animating principle inside. Divorce faith and works, and you have another corpse on your hands, a Christian corpse. Faith lies dead when there are no works. When there is no fruit and no evidence of saving faith flowing out of your fingertips and feet and running down your street, all the way down the road into your church, then James asks if your faith is alive or dead.

Here's the true nitty-gritty: Are we better at words than we are at embodying works? Do we *talk* a good game?

"And one of you says to them, 'Go in peace, be warmed and filled,' without giving them the things needed for the body" (2:16). Sometimes we love serving up words more than winter warmers, and speech more than soup. But when was the last time I gave something needed for the body of another believer? Christians must never think that it's just the soul that matters. If we ever think we are living only for a spiritual eternity, James wants to know what we had for breakfast this morning and what we plan to do about those who we know had none.

Are we better at theology than at anthropology? Do you *believe* a good game? Have all the right theology up there behind you on your shelves? If best practice is clearly laid out in our denominational book of church order, but there is no time to care practically, we can't presume that our faith is alive.

James himself gives us two practical examples to drive this point home.

"Was not Abraham our father justified by works when he offered up his son Isaac on the altar?" (2:21). The point is that trust in God always leads to obedience to God. Abraham believed God and was justified by faith alone, but that same trust led to the kind of obedience that showed he had a living and an active faith.

"And in the same way was not also Rahab the prostitute justified by works when she received the messengers and sent them out by another way?" (2:25). Rahab took in the messengers who arrived in her home; she protected and saved them, so you could actually see her faith. Her actions told you she was justified.

I think there's a deliberate reason why James chooses Rahab to illustrate his point. Trust in God always leads to service for God, shown in serving his people. James is interested in the realities of everyday life: those who are poorly clothed, cold, and hungry; those who need refuge and protection. They are here as examples, not as an exhaustive list. The paradigm is this: people with ability and resources helping the brother or sister with inability and no resources. The believer with plenty helping the believer in need. It is for us to reflect on this, and to rub the details into the corners of our lives.

Younger reader, do you know the physical needs of the older folks whom God has placed in your life? How do they get to church? Can they do their shopping? Are they lonely? In our heads we might say to ourselves that we know their needs, but James is asking if others can actually see what we say we know. Seeing is believing.

These are really whole-family questions. What would a "body-check" analysis reveal in your fellowship? I suspect that many needs go unnoticed not because we're unwilling to help but because we've stopped noticing. This would make James wonder if we have silently divorced our faith from our works and are not actively looking to display the faith we have.

A Word to the Complacent

One of the great tragic realities in pastoral ministry is that when a struggling, warring married couple sit with me in my study, it's often too late. They have been separating slowly over many years. They are now staring at the dead remains of their relationship and trying to find a way to verbalize the *D* word in front of each other and with me. Divorce might still lie ahead—or it might, in God's kindness, still be avoided—but they've been living together while pulling apart for ages.

Divorcing what God has joined can be like this. It creeps up on us unawares. Most of the time we don't realize, or have stopped realizing, that we live our lives divorcing what we believe about God from what God himself says that belief should look like. We say we have trust in God, but we do not have obedience toward God. James is saying that your disobedience is the real health check for your trust. I believe in Jesus, but I'm not obeying Jesus's words. James is saying that kind of belief is dead. Not real. Not saving.

We have to ask ourselves if there are parts of our lives where we know we are simply not obeying the voice of the Lord in his Scriptures but carrying on as if it doesn't really matter. If so, we are pulling apart what God has joined together and revealing death where we tell ourselves there is life. Jesus said that, at the end, many will profess their faith, only to be told they cannot enter the kingdom of heaven. The person who enters is "the one who does the will of my Father who is in heaven" (Matt. 7:21).

A Word to the Sensitive

I want to finish with a word to the tender conscience. Many of us are thinking by this point: "How do I know my faith is alive? How many good works are enough?" or, "I haven't clothed someone or fed someone, so am I a true Christian?"

We need to remember that this letter is written to churches very far down the road in the wrong direction. These are not believers seeking to do good works because of their love for the Lord Jesus; rather, they are professing believers in danger of abandoning even the attempt at good works. James knows, as much as we know, that you simply cannot do everything every time to everyone. God hasn't asked you to carry the whole church or the whole world on your shoulders.

But if all you ever do is turn a blind eye to need and distress, passing it on to someone else, there's a problem. You will know, as you read these lines, if you can feel your love for Christ pulling on your heart strings to be the kind of person who lives for him. By loving others. By obeying his word. By serving his people. When you feel yourself wanting to do these things, however imperfectly, however much you might be hindered by constraints like the age of your kids or the nature of your job, well, then the Lord knows you. It's not about how much or how often. It's about whether you've ever done these things at all, or intend to do them, or want to do them.

I suspect that for all of us right here and now there is something to change. Something to start. Maybe it will take time. But as love for Christ grows in our hearts, living faith in Christ just finds a way. It always finds a way. It just spills out.

Living faith just has a way of moving, walking, talking, and showing it's really alive.

Questions for Discussion or Personal Reflection

1. What are James's two warnings in this chapter? How have you seen these two temptations in your own life?

2. How would you summarize the way that James's view of faith and works sits alongside Paul's view of faith and works?

3. What do you think your neighbors on your street can see about your faith?

4. What do we need to know about the Lord Jesus in order to love and live like him?

5. Think and pray about how you handle your money, time, food, resources. Ask God to help you see the needs around you that you have been overlooking until now.

5

Words

In any situation there is the temptation to give in to a subtle egoism that gives you goose bumps at hearing yourself talk. The more you hear yourself, the less you can be taught by anyone but yourself.

R. KENT HUGHES, *JAMES: FAITH THAT WORKS*

[1] Not many of you should become teachers, my brothers, for you know that we who teach will be judged with greater strictness. [2] For we all stumble in many ways. And if anyone does not stumble in what he says, he is a perfect man, able also to bridle his whole body. [3] If we put bits into the mouths of horses so that they obey us, we guide their whole bodies as well. [4] Look at the ships also: though they are so large and are driven by strong winds, they are guided by a very small rudder wherever the will of the pilot directs. [5] So also the tongue is a small member, yet it boasts of great things.

How great a forest is set ablaze by such a small fire! [6] And the tongue is a fire, a world of unrighteousness. The tongue is set among our members, staining the whole body, setting on fire the entire course of life, and set on fire by hell. [7] For every kind of beast and bird, of reptile and sea creature, can be tamed and has been tamed by mankind, [8] but no human being can tame the tongue. It is a restless evil, full of deadly poison. [9] With it we bless our Lord and Father, and with it we curse people who are made in the likeness of God. [10] From the same mouth come blessing and cursing. My brothers, these things ought not to be so. [11] Does a spring pour forth from the same opening both fresh and salt water? [12] Can a fig tree, my brothers, bear olives, or a grapevine produce figs? Neither can a salt pond yield fresh water.

JAMES 3:1–12

"IN THE BEGINNING was the Word, and the Word was with God, and the Word was God. He was in the beginning with God. All things were made through him, and without him was not any thing made that was made" (John 1:1–3).

By his own Word, Jesus, God made everything. With his own words, he called the universe into existence, and so God has made a world in which words matter. Words can inflict the worst of evils or bestow the best of blessings.

At the Tokyo Olympics in 2021, the British public finally got to celebrate a gold medal performance in the men's diving competition. After years of expectation, Tom Daley and his partner triumphed in synchronized diving. But it was a victory in the face of personal heartache. When Daley and his partner came fourth at the London Olympics in 2012, a seventeen-year-old boy in Weymouth sent him this message on Twitter: "You let your dad down; I hope you know that." Tom's father, who had been his coach and biggest inspiration, had died of brain cancer just before those Olympic games.

"You let your dad down; I hope you know that."

A woman in Los Angeles who took her own life left just two words in her suicide note: "They said."

The book of Proverbs says,

Death and life are in the power of the tongue,
and those who love it will eat its fruits. (18:21)

When things go wrong, every time in every place, there will be words at work. Unravel it all, and you'll discover that someone said something. Someone sent an email. Someone texted. And carnage followed.

James chapter 3 is very like the book of Proverbs, because James loves graphic illustrations about our mouths, our words, and, in particular, our tongues. So, here in this chapter we will see three things James is saying about the tongue: it is small; it is a fire; it is a fountain. Then I want to show why he's making these observations and what we should do about them.

The Tongue Is Small—It Has Power out of All Proportion to Its Size

"For we all stumble in many ways. And if anyone does not stumble in what he says, he is a perfect man, able also to bridle his whole body. If we put bits into the mouths of horses so that they obey us, we guide their whole bodies as well" (James 3:2–3).

The tongue is tiny, but it's as if James is saying that it's the control room for the whole person, and yet it's the hardest part to control. Being self-controlled in what we say is one of the most difficult of disciplines, but if we can get that right, well, it will lead to a kind of integration and wholeness in the rest of life. James says tongue control makes "a perfect man" (3:2). If you can keep control of your tongue, then you can take control of the whole body. You think you've got wandering eyes or violent hands? Remarkably, James is actually encouraging us to change the kinds of things going on inside us that lead to the words we speak, and then we'll find the rest of our bodies falling in line behind. A very small thing controls a very big thing. James gives three illustrations: a tiny piece of equipment can guide the whole body of a mighty horse; a tiny rudder can guide a whole battleship; a tiny spark can set a great forest ablaze.

I think that James is also alerting us to how something so small in the body affects all the other ways in which the body works. We can see this by considering verbs from the rest of the Bible that make plain what the tongue can do. The tongue and its words can steal, conceal, store up, lift up, invite, cheer, crush, stir, spread, nourish, pierce, heal, endure, snare, satisfy, rebuke, harm, wound, hit, shoot, lie, flatter, boast, insult, divide, and slander. Just think of the extraordinary ways in which recipients of any of these actions from the tongue are affected by them. So, if you want to chart a path through life full of wholeness for you and for those you meet along the way, then the success of that journey is dependent on what you do with your tongue.

You possess a piece of flesh that is very small, but, out of all proportion to its size, its power is enormous.

The Tongue Is a Fire—It Can Destroy
out of All Proportion to Its Size

"How great a forest is set ablaze by such a small fire! And the tongue is a fire, a world of unrighteousness" (James 3:5–6). You are sitting reading this book with a weapon of mass destruction in your body.

Notice the details. The tongue is "a world of unrighteousness." This means that the tongue has its own ecosystem, which is devoted to everything that is wrong. It is the bodily representation of your inner dividedness. It is not just that the tongue is evil, but "it is a restless evil" (3:8). It can't sit still or be quiet. The tongue simply can't help itself, and inside it is poison. Like nicotine that stains the teeth, the tongue stains the whole body (3:6), and like venom in the nervous system, it permeates the whole body and can wound and maim as it shuts someone down, maybe irreversibly.

The tongue may be small, but just as a fire erupts from a spark, so the tongue can destroy out of all proportion to its size. It's like bacteria, or the Ebola or COVID-19 viruses; its damage can just spread and spread, and it cannot be tamed. The picture is so comprehensive. Beast and bird, reptile and mammal, land and sea, you name them: someone somewhere has taught a cobra to swing to music, and a lion to let his tamer stick his head in his jaws, and killer whales to carry children, and raptors to land on your outstretched hand. But no one, not even Solomon himself, not one single person, has ever learned how to get to the end of a single day and lay his head on his pillow without having reason to think: "Maybe I shouldn't have said that earlier. I probably should have expressed myself differently." No one dies without having thought that. Why not? Because you cannot tame the tongue.

I once saw someone split the top of her finger wide open with an axe. The pain and the damage were immense, and it was just her finger, a small part of the body. I've also seen people figuratively cut in two because of lies told about them. Reputations destroyed, careers ended, marriages traumatized because of untruthful words. I've watched whole churches engulfed in controversy because of one person's uncontrolled tongue, and all the calming words in the world couldn't seem to undo the angry words.

The imagery of taming here is so apt for the tongue because what is untamed is wild and dangerous and destructive. The tongue has the power to tear and pierce and paralyze and poison, like an axe separating a limb from the body, a sword separating flesh from the bone, or an intravenous drip of battery acid into the soul.

Think about some of the things we do with our tongues. Take gossip. It is an "acceptable" sin. James is dealing here with the effect of the tongue on the whole body and the way the tongue is motivated.

> The words of a whisperer are like delicious morsels;
>> they go down into the inner parts of the body. (Prov. 18:8)

That delicious little titbit of news that we just keep warm under the tongue for later. We love being in the know about something we don't really have a right to know but which gives us power. Few feelings match that kind of delight. Gossip is essentially inappropriate reports given to inappropriate people at inappropriate times. What is being said may actually be true—in fact, it's usually because we know it's true that we want to share it or receive it. Sometimes, though, we know it's not true. We spread rumors, a negative report about other people, or things based on uncertain evidence.

James says that, each and every time, the words that leave our mouths are setting things on fire.

Did you know that listening to gossip—not just speaking it—is a moral issue?

> An evildoer listens to wicked lips,
>> and a liar gives ear to a mischievous tongue. (Prov. 17:4)

It has been put like this: "Perhaps you don't have a problem with gossip yourself. But maybe you have that kind of welcoming face that attracts gossip to it." Others usually know whether gossip will get much airtime with us or not. The Bible says that if you pay close attention to slander, it makes you a liar too. The tongue has power to dehumanize not just the speaker but also the listener.

All of this has a positive counterpart. For James is saying that you can change the world today.

I used to watch our children make objects out of modeling clay. With their fingers, they would mold a formless blob into different shapes. They would cut and stick and press, and something new was born. We do that to each other with our words. We each go through life with the capacity to be molded or misshapen by the words of others that land on our ears. All the time we are being pressed or pulled, and harmed or healed, because of the penetrating power of words.

It is possible for someone to reach the end of this day in a far worse condition because of the words you send that person's way. It is also possible today to leave someone in significantly better shape because of something you might say to him or her.

The Tongue Is a Fountain—What It Produces Is in Perfect Harmony with Its Source

"With [the tongue] we bless our Lord and Father, and with it we curse people who are made in the likeness of God. From the same mouth come blessing and cursing" (James 3:9–10).

Morning worship for our Trinity Church family is usually over by 11:45 a.m. each Sunday. Most of us are back home an hour or so later. James knows that it's perfectly possible within the space of that hour to disown the faith we have just confessed. Maybe it happens even quicker than that; maybe it takes a little longer. It is possible to open our mouths to bless God in the closing song, shut them, smile, and go on our way, but then open the same mouths to utter words that castigate and criticize and tear down. Have you ever done that? Would people be amazed at the Sunday-afternoon you compared with the Sunday-morning you?

Look at James's logic. We're capable of speaking well of God one minute, but then, the next minute, saying things that destroy the very worth and dignity of people made in God's image.

I'm ashamed to admit it, but in one of the pandemic lockdowns the biggest argument between my wife and me occurred at home one Sunday during our online church service. Yes, during it—you read that right. Straight after saying the confession of sin together as a family, we actually started arguing over whether the person leading was saying the prayer too fast or too slow. Of course, we weren't really arguing over that: something trivial ignited underlying tensions, and whoosh, out it all came. Right in front of our kids. It is so embarrassing to recall that morning, though it gave our children a lot of amusement when we both had to say "sorry" to them later on for what they had witnessed. It was truly awful. "From the same mouth come blessing and cursing" (3:10).

As always, James's words here cut so very deep. For he is not just saying that one mouth can produce two opposite sets of words; more than this, it's that the two opposite kinds of speech reveal a corruption at the source. What comes out of our mouths is in perfect harmony with what lies beneath, at the bottom of the well. "Does a spring pour forth from the same opening both fresh and salt water? Can a fig tree, my brothers, bear olives, or a grapevine produce figs? Neither can a salt pond yield fresh water" (3:11–12). Our words reveal our hearts. If the words aren't fresh, then the heart is not healthy. Our speech is a window into our souls; it shines a light on what is going on beneath the surface.

Craig Troxel says that the eyes and ears are the gatekeepers of our hearts, and our tongues are our hearts' ambassadors. What we have laid up in our hearts cannot stay in there. "All of it comes gushing out. Whatever is stored there, whether good treasure or bad, will be published by our mouth."[1] That is a powerful image: the tongue is the heart's publisher. The Lord Jesus said, "Out of the abundance of the heart his mouth speaks" (Luke 6:45). What's inside me cannot be kept inside me.

If I have a big heart, then you will hear patient words.

If I have a bruised heart, you'll hear hurting and hurtful words.

If I have an empty heart, you'll hear loud but hollow words.

If I have a wise heart, you will hear sound words.

James knows that if our hearts are divided, the words that come out are divided. A wonderful way to picture it (though not original to me) is like this: Your tongue is the hinge on which the door of your heart swings. When you speak, you open your heart wide to the world.

Don't ever think that you've got "the real you" deep inside, somehow kept invisible and separate from all the words you are speaking. Who we are as people is much more visible to others than we may realize, and it is all displayed in the kinds of words we speak.

So, let me suggest a range of ways we can begin to respond to this. At each stage, as we work our way through James, we want to allow his words to work on our hearts.

Take Your Words to God

Never try to fix your words by mending your mouth. Instead, the heart needs to change. Since the tongue is the hinge on which the door of the heart turns, we need to open our hearts to God first of all, and then when we open our mouths, things will be different. A heart that is right before God is what creates the mouth of the righteous and leads to the words of the wise.

"But he gives more grace. Therefore it says, 'God opposes the proud but gives grace to the humble.' Submit yourselves therefore to God" (James 4:6–7). The epistle of James is a world of grace for us. Like me, you are the owner of words let loose in the world and in the lives of others. We all own words we're proud of and would say again if we could; and we all have our names attached to words we would give absolutely anything to unsay and take back. But James reminds us that God's words to us matter more than any other words to us. No words have ever come from your mouth that cannot be conquered by words from his mouth. There is nothing you have said that cannot be forgiven and wiped clean in God's sight, even if here on earth the consequences remain. There is nothing that others have said to you for which God is unwilling to forgive them. The doors in our hearts must always stay open to forgiveness.

All of this comes from seeing yourself and the world and your words in the light of God's words. The humility of your heart—or the independence and self-reliance of your heart—is always the fountain for your words, and there is only one place where we ever change that fountain: on our knees before God.

Set Your Words to Work

Do you ever consciously and deliberately set your words to work, sending them off into the world and into someone else's life to do them good? James is picturing for us a world of people who, because they belong to a speaking God, are intentional speakers.

I don't think his images of fresh water and olives, figs, and grapes are coincidental. Like the book of Proverbs, James is showing us that words can give life.

> From the fruit of a man's mouth his stomach is satisfied;
>   he is satisfied by the yield of his lips.
> Death and life are in the power of the tongue,
>   and those who love it will eat its fruits. (Prov. 18:20–21)

Are you hungry to eat the food your own words have created?

Stop and think about it. When was the last time you built something with your words? Or tried to change something with your speech? Or harvested something because of words you'd deliberately sown a long time before? I think we harvest our words all the time, probably way more than we realize. But don't just let it happen to you, as if you've got absolutely no control. Plant your words somewhere and watch how powerful they are.

Don't Rush to Teach

Did you notice the words that open James chapter 3? "Not many of you should become teachers, my brothers, for you know that we who teach will be judged with greater strictness" (3:1).

This whole passage about speech and the tongue comes because of a warning to those who want to teach others, a necessary warning when words are in the mix.

A few years ago, a GoFundMe campaign took off all over the United Kingdom. The general population crowdfunded an effort to put on billboards all the things our politicians had said about Brexit which then came back to haunt them. The then British prime minister, David Cameron, said that the electorate faced a simple choice: "Stability and strong government with me, or chaos with Ed Miliband." It is hard to underestimate how foolish those words looked as the United Kingdom careered through the instability and seemingly endless confusion of the Brexit process, albeit without David Cameron. The words we speak and the tweets we post and the emails we send are all out there, and we can't get them back. In my Gmail I have an "undo" feature, which allows me to recall an email up to thirty seconds after I've clicked "send." This has saved my bacon a few times. But it only lasts for thirty seconds.

It's one thing to say something you regret, but if you're a leader, a public teacher—oh, the power, the devastating power of your words. Neville Chamberlain famously declared, "Peace for our time," but within months Europe was plunged into World War II.

James is saying that there's something worse than these misspoken words that echo down through time: it is the Bible teacher whose tongue is not under control. This is a very sobering reality. For if the tongue is not controlled, then other things will not be controlled, and if the tongue is not controlled, then a church leader can do extraordinary damage.

When I was much younger, I used to think that if I learned to teach the Bible, I would then be able to lead a church. I wanted to master a set of exegetical and theological skills to set me on my way. It was a noble aim. Then God in his kindness gave me a wife, and then kids, and then a church and fellow elders. I have come to realize over time that learning to speak the Bible's words is one part of the task, and learning to be self-controlled in my words is another vital part. In all of the good relational gifts God has given me, I've realized that he has been working on my heart and on who I am as a man before him. He has given me several different forums where my words can reveal so much about me. It's as if God has been saying to me over the years: "Never mind the teaching. Shall we just take a look inside? Let's just look at your heart."

Do you want to lead and preach? Do you want to teach one day? Then remember, "We who teach will be judged with greater strictness" (3:1). This is all because of the responsibility that comes with the task. As R. Kent Hughes points out, James knows that evil ambitions motivate some to teach, and "if such people got into teaching positions, they would suffer further corruption because teaching offices are fraught with moral dangers of their own."[2] The love of the Lord Jesus for his people burns so brightly precisely because of false shepherds who do not feed his people but rather fleece them. The fire of the Old Testament prophets burned most fiercely against the shepherds in Israel who were abusing and harming the flock instead of protecting them (see Ezek. 34).

And yet we must notice God's grace even here. James is not saying that teachers must be perfect. "For we all stumble in many ways" (3:2).

May I ask if you have grace for your teachers and for those who labor in the word of God for you? I ask this as a minister who knows what it is like to be on the receiving end of harsh words. Your pastor will know this well. A pulpit can be one of the loneliest places on earth. Sometimes those who lead you by speaking to you will stumble because of what they say. James is a model of grace toward them.

No one can tame the tongue. I will blow it, and you will blow it; and James manages to say in one breath that we all stumble (3:2), and in the next breath, "My brothers, these things ought not to be so" (3:10).

It might be worth simply finishing this chapter with some intentional reflection on how you, personally, are going to work these things out in your life. James will also later tell us, "Do not speak evil against one another, brothers" (4:11). Maybe there's a relationship that's been broken by words spoken against another—whether to you or by you—but you know you can bring about at least some restoration by changing your speech. Apparently, each person speaks, on average, sixteen thousand words a day.[3] How many of them are *against* someone else?

I presume we can all agree that there is something about social media that feeds that word "against." The existence of Twitter means that never before have so many with so little to say said so much so recklessly. But Twitter's greatest problem is that it is a world of haughty eyes and lying lips, a festering pit of posture problems, a competitive arena where we seek to look superior or vie for fleeting affirmation. All these sins are so often on display. Social media demands quick reactions to everything. It is very hard to love our neighbors as ourselves on social media.

> When words are many, transgression is not lacking,
>   but whoever restrains his lips is prudent. (Prov. 10:19)

> If one gives an answer before he hears,
>   it is his folly and shame. (Prov. 18:13)

But it is often just as hard in the real world as in the virtual world.

We should notice in James where all the action takes place. It's all within a family—brothers, sisters, a church family—that's where we speak against one another. This helps us to think about the way we speak at home. It's easy to be growing as Christians but to neglect spiritual graces within our own families.

Husbands and wives: Of the words you have spoken today, how many have been against your spouse, and how many for him or her?

Young folks to parents: it's easy to think, "It's just Mom and Dad, so I can speak to them however I like." How many of your words are against them, either in their presence or out of earshot?

Parents to children: We must not sit above God's law in our words. We must never give our children less than God's law in our speech, and that will teach us to give them so much more as well: we will be gentle, kind, compassionate, gracious, merciful, and forgiving in the way that we speak.

Gracious words are like a honeycomb,
    sweetness to the soul and health to the body. (Prov. 16:24)

The tongue of the righteous is choice silver. (Prov. 10:20)

A gentle tongue is a tree of life,
    but perverseness in it breaks the spirit. (Prov. 15:4)

An honest answer
    is like a kiss on the lips. (Prov. 24:26 NIV)

A word fitly spoken
    is like apples of gold in a setting of silver. (Prov. 25:11)

The lips of the righteous feed many. (Prov. 10:21)

It is amazing how many times good words are connected to good eating. James wonders, as you read these lines, if anyone is getting nourished at your table today. This very day you will spread, or you have already spread, a banquet of words for others to consume. Is it feast or famine? Is it poison or life-giving balm? Who are you going to speak about in new ways, gracious ways, forgiving ways? Who are you going to encourage? Text, email, tweet, message, write, or call?

As you read these lines, is there something in you, something about to be said by you, that ought not to be? Take it to God.

Has someone said something to you that he or she ought not to have? Take it to God.

James knows what ought to be: words from our mouths that teach with godly instruction and humility, words that shape and direct and cause the kind of flourishing in others we long to see grow in our own hearts too.

Our words ought to produce fruit, bring health, bestow beauty, sow in righteousness, and reveal the wisdom from above.

Questions for Discussion or Personal Reflection

1. How have you personally seen the power of the tongue both to give life and to destroy?

2. Why must we deal with our hearts in order to deal with our words?

3. "The tongue is the heart's publisher." What do you think God is saying to you in his word about the kind of publisher you are?

4. Are you more tempted to speak gossip or to listen to it? Why?

5. In what ways could you set out a feast with your words, even today?

6

Wisdom

Christianity is the religion of the broken heart.

J. GRESHAM MACHEN, *CHRISTIANITY AND LIBERALISM*

[13] Who is wise and understanding among you? By his good conduct let him show his works in the meekness of wisdom. [14] But if you have bitter jealousy and selfish ambition in your hearts, do not boast and be false to the truth. [15] This is not the wisdom that comes down from above, but is earthly, unspiritual, demonic. [16] For where jealousy and selfish ambition exist, there will be disorder and every vile practice. [17] But the wisdom from above is first pure, then peaceable, gentle, open to reason, full of mercy and good fruits, impartial and sincere. [18] And a harvest of righteousness is sown in peace by those who make peace.

[1] What causes quarrels and what causes fights among you? Is it not this, that your passions are at war within you? [2] You desire and do not have, so you murder. You covet and cannot obtain, so you fight and quarrel. You do not have, because you do not ask. [3] You ask and do not receive, because you ask wrongly, to spend it on your passions. [4] You adulterous people! Do you not know that friendship with the world is enmity with God? Therefore whoever wishes to be a friend of the world makes himself an

enemy of God. ⁵ Or do you suppose it is to no purpose that the Scripture says, "He yearns jealously over the spirit that he has made to dwell in us"? ⁶ But he gives more grace. Therefore it says, "God opposes the proud but gives grace to the humble." ⁷ Submit yourselves therefore to God. Resist the devil, and he will flee from you. ⁸ Draw near to God, and he will draw near to you. Cleanse your hands, you sinners, and purify your hearts, you double-minded. ⁹ Be wretched and mourn and weep. Let your laughter be turned to mourning and your joy to gloom. ¹⁰ Humble yourselves before the Lord, and he will exalt you.

¹¹ Do not speak evil against one another, brothers. The one who speaks against a brother or judges his brother, speaks evil against the law and judges the law. But if you judge the law, you are not a doer of the law but a judge. ¹² There is only one lawgiver and judge, he who is able to save and to destroy. But who are you to judge your neighbor?

JAMES 3:13–4:12

WHAT DO YOU HATE?

Broccoli. Being cold, or being hot. Working nights. Snow. Wind. Heights. Mushrooms. The last day of camp. The end of the holidays. Mushy peas. Tax returns. Choosing the wrong queue in the supermarket.

What do you hate?

Take it up a notch. Your car left damaged in the supermarket parking lot with no culprit in sight. Rising energy costs and property and school taxes. The meager value of your pension. Getting old. Still working at sixty-five.

What do you hate?

Sexual abuse. Child abuse. Racism. Abortion. Discrimination. Daily unfairness and gross injustice. Death. The good dying young from cancer and the wicked living long into old age.

Spread out across a spectrum, our hates range from bad to worse, and yet not one of them comes close to the thing that God hates most: pride.

We know that God detests sin and evil, but God's hatred of pride is everywhere in the Bible. That hatred for pride is pure, it is holy, and it burns with white-hot intensity.

> There are six things that the LORD hates,
> seven that are an abomination to him. (Prov. 6:16)

Number one on the list is "haughty eyes" (Prov. 6:17). Literally, the phrase is "a rising pair of eyes." We talk about raised *eyebrows* for surprise; the Bible talks about raised *eyes* for pride. The prophet Isaiah says, "When the Lord has finished all his work on Mount Zion and on Jerusalem, he will punish the speech of the arrogant heart of the king of Assyria and the boastful look in his eyes" (Isa. 10:12). These are the eyes of the pompous invader, the proud king, the person who belongs in the domain of creatures but who elevates himself to the place of divine majesty, where he does not belong. And it is no little thing when the creature rises up to where only the Creator belongs. God's reaction to this in his own people is especially strong. He hates it (Amos 6:8).

In this chapter, we are going to consider James's antidote to the proud heart. In a phrase, it is "the meekness of wisdom" (3:13). This whole letter is about getting wise. It is wisdom for foolish Christians and foolish churches, and if we want to fix what ails us, we don't just need to fix our words or our actions, but we must also recalibrate our hearts with wisdom.

When things go wrong in a church, or in the world, we so often look for quick solutions. Do A, not B; stop doing that; start doing this. We look for actions that will fix things, but it is James's settled conviction that outward actions need to flow from a wise heart: "Who is wise and understanding among you? By his good conduct let him show his works in the meekness of wisdom" (3:13).

That's right at the beginning of our passage, and right at the end James tells us that pride is such a big deal to God that we need to destroy it before it destroys us, and run from it in all its forms. "But he gives more grace. Therefore it says, 'God opposes the proud but gives grace to the humble'" (4:6). This leads to a clear command: "Humble yourselves before the Lord, and he will exalt you" (4:10).

So, meek wisdom and humble relationship to God are our theme in this chapter. They are what the medicine of the gospel looks like in our lives as we seek to heal our inner fractured selves. Without wisdom, we will foolishly continue to speak and act in ways fundamentally at odds with who we know we should be; without humility, we will constantly show ourselves to be out of step with the Lord of glory, to whom we say we belong.

In the Christian worldview, wisdom is an ethical category before it is ever an intellectual, or even a practical, category. It has to do with the kind of persons we are before God. It is a beautiful truth, expressed by Hannah Anderson, that "wisdom is ultimately an outgrowth of humility. Becoming wise people, becoming people who can make good decisions only comes when we understand who God is and who we are as a result."[1] If we humble ourselves before the Lord, our souls grow the kind of invigorating wisdom that nourishes our wholeness.

James presents us with four divisions in the passage to help us examine where we stand. In which of these domains have we made our home? On which side of the line do we stand? What kind of relational posture toward others do we assume?

Division 1: Between Above and Below

James has already referred to the wisdom that God gives (1:5), and he says that such a gift comes "from above" (1:17). Now, in 3:13–18, James develops this spatial imagery by saying there is a division between above and below, between two different ways of living; and although he doesn't explicitly call it this, it's a division between two different types of wisdom.

There is a way of being in the world that is shaped by heaven itself: "The wisdom from above is first pure, then peaceable, gentle, open to reason, full of mercy and good fruits, impartial and sincere" (3:17). In stark contrast, there is a way of living in the world that is shaped from below, which is "earthly, unspiritual." This type of "wisdom" is actually "demonic" (3:15).

Notice the fracture. Sense how high and wide the divide. The beauty of the wisdom from above is set over against the ugliness and horror of that which is from below: "Where jealousy and selfish ambition exist, there will be disorder and every vile practice" (3:16). Yet, in opposition to disorder there can be a harvest: "And a harvest of righteousness is sown in peace by those who make peace" (3:18).

Again, as in so many other places, James's vision of human flourishing mirrors closely the teaching of Jesus in the Sermon on the Mount: "Blessed are the peacemakers, for they shall be called sons of God" (Matt. 5:9). There is a way to be like God, and that is to do what God does and treat others with lavish grace and merciful condescension. Indeed, the command to "be perfect, as your heavenly Father is perfect" (Matt. 5:48) follows immediately after the command to love your enemies, for that is what will make you "sons of your Father who is in heaven" (5:44–45).

God himself treats those who are opposed to him in the most radically generous of ways, and that is the very atmosphere of the letter of James. The divisions that exist between people, good and bad, must not lead to divided actions in the heart and mind of the follower of Jesus, as if we are to treat some with kindness and some with disdain. Instead, we show that our hearts are wholly committed to God by being the kind of people who, because of the gospel and through the gospel, try to do everything we can to live at peace with all.

When Ben Traynor, our ministry trainee, preached this passage at Trinity, he captivated us with an illustration about an older gentleman who attended the church where Ben had grown up in Edinburgh.[2] Ben was eight years old when he first met this man, and only in his teens did Ben discover that the man was a well-known Christian who had many books to his name, had pastored a healthy church, and had led a significant and influential ministry. Ben had only a few conversations with this man, but the gentleman left an enormous impression on Ben in a way that was hard to articulate—that is, until Ben came to James 3:13–18. All of a sudden he realized he was looking at a portrait of this older saint. He left the impression of wisdom and godliness. All the attributes of wisdom from above flowed out of him, even down to a little, insignificant schoolboy in the congregation. The man was pure, not in the sense of being sinless but in the sense of being so wholly devoted to God in love that he was able to be devoted to others in love. He was gentle, able to stoop to others who had nothing of worth to give him in return. He was sincere. He did not live one life on a ministry platform that was different from his life among God's people, in all their variety.

Division 2: Between God and the World

Although James's language is strong at the end of chapter 3, it is nothing compared with the intensity of the first ten verses of chapter 4. We began this book by focusing on the issue of adultery, which is at the heart of these verses. In many ways, here we touch the very nerve center of James's vision of the double-minded believer, and its opposite as seen in the humble and repentant believer.

Division is present in almost every line. Believers are divided from each other in fights and quarrels. Believers are in turmoil in their inner beings with "passions . . . at war within" them (4:1). Sinful desires cannot be realized, which in turn leads to a further escalation of conflict (4:2). Here are people divided between having and asking—either not asking God at all or asking him for the wrong things (4:2–3). And in it all, this behavior is in stark contrast to Abraham in chapter 2, who was called a friend of God precisely because his faith was alive and active, as shown in his faithful works (2:22–23). Here, however, believers are not friends with God but friends with the world even as they profess allegiance to God. Christians who live like this—saying one thing to God but embracing behaviors that belong to his enemies and do not resemble him—are adulterers.

We have seen this so clearly already in James that I don't think I need to belabor the point. Instead, I want to say more about God's glorious, gracious response. From 4:5 onward, it is clear that James wants us to know that God's response to the unfaithfulness of his people is as stunningly unexpected today as ever it was throughout the centuries when his old covenant people wandered off and

on every high hill
      and under every green tree
      . . . bowed down like a whore. (Jer. 2:20)

The language of the prophets, and of James, is so strong precisely because the sin is so awful, so tragic, which is what makes God's response so spectacular: "Do you suppose it is to no purpose that the Scripture says, 'He yearns jealously over the spirit that he has made to dwell in us'?" (James 4:5). This is not the language of rejection, which is what adultery rightly deserves, but the language of jealous love finding a way to make the relationship whole again.

The word "jealously" should make us sit up and take notice. When "jealousy" is used to describe us, it is used negatively; it depicts a world of selfish self-preservation: "bitter jealousy" (3:14). But here "jealously" describes how God himself yearns, so it cannot be an expression of anything sinful in his perfect being. Rather, it is a measure of his loving ownership of us and the reality of his union to us in Jesus through his indwelling Spirit. We are *his*—precisely the thing that makes our sin so terrible but his love so incredible. He will not let us go. He loves us in a way that makes him able and willing to forgive our sins and to welcome us back: "But he gives more grace" (4:6).

James's call to repent, to return to a gracious God despite our waywardness, reminds me of the beauty of Jesus's parable of the two lost sons (Luke 15:11–32). The younger son gives us a picture of repentance realized, of proper and correct self-assessment and return to God, whereas the elder son, no less lost, gives us a picture of proud-hearted refusal to accept God's gracious favor. A family divides into two different responses to grace: running toward it or rejecting it.

The attitude of the younger son is exactly what James wants us to adopt here. Luke tells us that the son "came to himself" (15:17). It's a way of saying that he came to his senses and realized his duplicity. Repentance happens in that moment when you find yourself almost looking at yourself, and you can see the fracture in your soul as if you were looking at it from the outside. It's the moment when you question: "What was I thinking? How did I do that?" It's why James invites you to "purify your hearts, you double-minded" (4:8). Make your split soul whole again. We do this by recognizing that we have done wrong.

The younger son confesses, "I have sinned against heaven and before you" (Luke 15:21). Repentance is saying what is true. "Cleanse your hands, you sinners" (James 4:8). This means repentance is so simple, and yet so hard. I have sinned. No qualifications, no excuses, no attachments, no carefully managed media statement. The younger son doesn't think he needs therapy, but rather rescue, a restored relationship.

Repentance is not saying, "I'm sorry if . . ." Any time you add the little word "if" to your apology, to your repentance, it is not true repentance.

"I'm sorry if I hurt you."

"I'm sorry if you're upset by what I did."

"If" transfers responsibility away from you and puts it back on the one you're speaking to, and in so doing, it guts the apology of true efficacy. But true repentance is knowing that what we did was wrong, and saying so without anyone else having to pull the strings. End of story. No *ifs*, no *buts*, no *maybes*. God loves it when we say what is true about ourselves, out in the light, no shadows, no camouflage, no fig leaves. The whole point is that it is precisely this attitude that paves a return into the open arms of our heavenly

Father: "Draw near to God, and he will draw near to you" (4:8). For this kind of humility, a world of grace awaits.

I will say more about this later.

Division 3: Between You and Your Fellow Christian

Pride is all about posture. Haughtiness is highness; humility is lowness. We can see that explicitly in James 4:10: if we abase ourselves, God will exalt us, and when we are not humble in our relationships, our posture is wrong. Look at the posture word in verse 11: "Do not speak evil *against* one another." One of the ways to measure how humble you are is to count how many people you are against in your words.

> There are six things that the Lord hates,
> seven that are an abomination to him. (Prov. 6:16)

Number one, as I have said, is "haughty eyes," and number two is "a lying tongue" (Prov. 6:17). It is not accidental that one follows the other, for pride of the eyes leads to deceit in the tongue. Pride in the divided heart will come out in the evil of divided words. It just will.

The word "evil" isn't in the Greek text of James 4:11. The phrase is simply "Do not speak against one another," and that can take so many different forms. We can speak evil of one another; we can say things that are untrue or unkind, and so they're against someone. But it is just as easy to say true things about someone as a form of speaking against them. Maybe when we say, "Have you heard such and such about so and so?" Every word is true, and yet it is against someone. So, you can speak evil by speaking the truth—it's just truth you should be keeping entirely to yourself, and it doesn't need to be said. Your true words are pushing against a brother or sister.

You can speak evil when you slander someone or when you flatter someone. The famous description of the difference between slander and flattery is so helpful: slander is saying behind someone's back what we'd never say to her face, and flattery is saying to someone's face what we'd never say behind her back. Both kinds of speech are against others.

Who is James addressing here? Look at the word he uses: "brothers" (4:11). What is a family for? Arms linked. Beside. Around. For. With. Not *against*. Dear reader, not against. "Do not speak against one another."

Abstract theological ideas are all well and good, and we all know what it's like to keep big Bible concepts at arm's length so that they don't actually interfere with our lives. Don't be proud. Be humble. "Great. Got it. Thanks, James," we might say. "I look forward to next week's sermon." But, as we've been learning, James just won't let us do that.

The book of James is a bit like having a member of the welcome team at church stop you at the door as you leave and ask you directly: "So, tell me, what are you going to change today? 'Do not boast and be false to the truth' (3:14). 'God opposes the proud but gives grace to the humble' (4:6). What are you actually going to do to about these things?"

"Well, look, I'm kind of new here, and this is a bit intense . . ."

"No, tell me, what are you going to change?"

Your inquisitor pins you to the coffee table—smiling—ever so forcefully.

That awkward welcome team member is James, for he just keeps reminding us that humility takes real concrete form in the words you're about to speak to someone over coffee, or to another person when you get behind the wheel of your car. The wisdom from above or the selfish ambition from below is concretely present when you get your calendar out tomorrow morning, and when you check your bank balance over lunch. *That's* where true religion lives, in all those nooks and crannies in our lives.

Division 4: Between You and God's Law

James builds on this immediately in 4:11. Your brother is not the only person you're speaking against.

Think of what it's like to be facing the school bully in the playground while knowing you have a big brother a couple of years above you. You're being picked on in third grade, and the bully doesn't know you've got a big brother in sixth grade. Eventually, maybe with knees knocking, you get to say to the bully: "If you're against me, you're also against him. And you really don't want to go up against him."

James wants us to conceive of every person we speak against as having something else attached to them, and if you're against that person, you're also against this other thing. "The one who speaks against a brother or judges his brother, speaks evil against the law and judges the law" (4:11). We need to remember what James means by this to see just why it is so hard-hitting: "If you really fulfill the royal law according to the Scripture, 'You shall love your neighbor as yourself,' you are doing well" (James 2:8). If you are speaking evil of your neighbor, then you are against your neighbor, and that means you're against the law and, ultimately, against God himself. You are saying that God's good law, which tells me that I should love you and not speak against you, is evil. And worse than that, if you speak evil against the law, you are judging the law. To set ourselves above the law of God is a posture problem like no other.

Many years ago in Belfast I was a passenger in a car being driven by a friend. I pointed out to him that he was doing more than forty miles per hour in a thirty-miles-per-hour zone. "I know," he said, "but I do it every day; I do it all the time. If I get stopped by the police, I plan to tell them this stretch of the road really should be forty miles per hour—they've got to make that change. It makes no sense to be a thirty zone."

How would you rate my friend's chances as the lights flash behind him and he prepares for a conversation with the uniformed officer? Pretty slim, in my book.

We can't judge the law; we simply have to do the law. We have to obey it. James couldn't be clearer that this is all a matter of posture. "If you judge the law, you are not a doer of the law but a judge" (4:11). Where does the judge sit in the courtroom? Up high. Above you. The law is above you, and you are beneath it.

Consider a really beautiful feature of God's law that may not be automatically obvious but is of the very essence of the law: when the Bible forbids one thing, it promotes its opposite.

"Do not murder" means love life.

"Lead me not into temptation" means lead me into righteousness.

"Do not commit adultery" means cherish and love marital faithfulness.

"Do not speak against one another" means, well, it's obvious: speak for, speak to, speak with, speak good of one another and well of each other.

The point is that unless we are actually doing the opposite of the thing prohibited, then we might be keeping the letter of the law, but we have not seen its animating principle, which is a life of love lived in complete obedience to the God who gave it.

A delightful example of this deep understanding of God's holy law appears in the Westminster Larger Catechism. The ninth commandment of the Decalogue is "You shall not bear false witness against your neighbor" (Ex. 20:16). In a quite remarkable way, the catechism climbs inside what this means.

Q. 144. *What are the duties required in the ninth commandment?*

A. The duties required in the ninth commandment are, the preserving and promoting of truth between man and man, and the good name of our neighbour, as well as our own; appearing and standing for the truth; and from the heart, sincerely, freely, clearly, and fully, speaking the truth, and only the truth, in matters of judgment and justice, and in all other things whatsoever; a charitable esteem of our neighbours; loving, desiring, and rejoicing in their good name; sorrowing for and covering of their infirmities; freely acknowledging of their gifts and graces, defending their innocency; a ready receiving of a good report, and unwillingness to admit of an evil report, concerning them; discouraging talebearers, flatterers, and slanderers; love and care of our own good name, and defending it when need requireth; keeping of lawful promises; studying and practicing of whatsoever things are true, honest, lovely, and of good report.[3]

And this is just one example from one of the commandments! It is quite something to realize that when we actively disobey the command of God's law and passively neglect the duties required by it, then we are putting ourselves above God's law.

"Love your neighbor as yourself."

"Yes, I hear those words, but if I get stopped by God in the road one day, I plan to tell him that particular neighbor is a stretch too far."

Observe where James has taken us: from the same level as a brother to being against him, then above him, and now right up there above even God.

When God says, "Love your neighbor as yourself," he has the right to say it, and he has the right to say that action is the best thing for me and for him or her. Who am I to say to God: "No, thanks. You take a seat, Your Honor. I'll decide!" Who am I to take the place of God and judge my neighbor? The very essence of pride is deicide. Killing God. Replacing God. It is the ultimate coup, the definitive act of rebellion—not just tearing up the rule book, the law, but replacing the one who gave it.

A famous actor was once given a private tour of Buckingham Palace. Allegedly, when shown the royal throne room, he posed for pictures of himself seated on Her Majesty's throne. It was a staggering breach of royal protocol. What did he have as he spied the throne? Haughty eyes.

What distinctive features did Adam and Eve possess in the garden, as they tasted the forbidden fruit? Rising eyes.

We lift ourselves up high, and God hates it. His glory is taken and shared with another.

Come Back, Again, to Jesus

The only person with the right to judge my neighbor is God. That's what James says: "There is only one lawgiver and judge" (4:12). God is the only person with a divine right to judge me. And yet, what has God done with me? Has he treated me as my sins deserve, or with grace and mercy?

Think of all the ways God could have spoken against you. He is the God of truth; he cannot speak evil and can say only what is true. We know that. But what if God were to speak out loud everything true about you for me to hear. Maybe a lot of it would entail speaking against you. It certainly would be so if God were to proclaim the truth about me. All my thoughts, sins, and pride—all spoken out loud. It would be a crushing wall of shame and guilt.

Here is the gospel of grace: God doesn't speak about us in humiliating ways to others, ever. Instead, he forgives our sins; he covers over our offenses; he has a bottomless sea of grace and mercy. All our sins and offenses are taken to Calvary and punished and paid for and done away with in the death of the Lord Jesus. He buries them in the ocean of his forgetfulness. He gives grace to humble, penitent sinners. The Judge becomes a Savior, a friend, a brother.

Compare this with what we do. We take our neighbor's sins and pick through them, raking them over, and then speak them out loud. We take secret delight in airing other people's dirty laundry for all to see.

James wants to know just who we think we are. Judge or brother? In reality, we make such poor judges, such harsh critics, and such unforgiving neighbors. It is so true, as Miroslav Volf has said, that "forgiveness flounders because . . . I exclude myself from the community of sinners."[4]

Maybe the best thing you can do as you read these things is simply wonder and adore, for God has taken the truth about you and let the Lord Jesus pay for it all in his death on the cross. Humility grows from here. It comes from the grace of God to us in Jesus. You cannot change your words without killing pride. And you cannot kill your pride while staying far away from Christ. So, humble yourself before the Lord, and he will exalt you.

Do you know the wonderful story of the funeral service for Otto von Habsburg, the last crown prince of Austria? After his death in 2011, his remains were borne to the Imperial Crypt of the Capuchin Church in Vienna. He was carried there to lie with his ancestors. During the funeral procession of a member of the imperial family, a dialogue takes place at the entrance to the church:

The Master of Ceremonies knocks on the door three times.

PRIOR: Who desires entry?

MC: Otto of Austria; once Crown Prince of Austria-Hungary; Royal Prince of Hungary and Bohemia, of Dalmatia, Croatia, Slavonia, Galicia, Lodomeria and Illyria; Grand Duke of Tuscany and Cracow; Duke of Lorraine, Salzburg, Styria, Carinthia, Carniola and the Bukowina; Grand Prince of Transylvania, Margrave of Moravia; Duke of Upper and Lower Silesia, of Modena, Parma, Piacenza, Guastalla, of Oświęcim and Zator, Teschen, Friaul, Dubrovnik and Zadar; Princely Count of Habsburg and Tyrol, of Kyburg, Gorizia and Gradisca; Prince of Trent and Brixen; Margrave of Upper and Lower Lusatia and Istria; Count of Hohenems, Feldkirch, Bregenz, Sonnenburg etc.; Lord of Trieste, Kotor and Windic March, Grand Voivod of the Voivodeship of Serbia, and so on.

PRIOR: We do not know him.

The MC knocks three times again.

PRIOR: Who desires entry?

MC: Dr Otto von Habsburg, President and Honorary President of the Paneuropean Union, Member and quondam President of the European Parliament, honorary doctor of many universities, honorary citizen of many cities in Central Europe, member of numerous venerable academies and institutes, recipient of high civil and ecclesiastical honours, awards and medals, which were given him in recognition of his decades-long struggle for the freedom of peoples for justice and right.

PRIOR: We do not know him.

The MC knocks three more times.

PRIOR: Who desires entry?

MC: Otto, a mortal and sinful man.

PRIOR: Then let him come in.[5]

There is a way to view ourselves—not just in death but in all of life—which will make us whole.

Questions for Discussion or Personal Reflection

1. Is it a surprise to you that God hates pride so much? What reasons does James give for that?

2. Can you think of concrete ways in which pride has shown itself recently in your words or actions?

3. Why does being "against" a brother or sister mean you have judged God's law?

4. How does the gospel of grace humble us?

5. In your own words, explain how God is different from us in the way that he speaks to us.

7

Presumption

If someone had told me when I was twenty years old
that life was very short and would pass—just like
that—I wouldn't have believed it. And if I tell you that,
you don't believe it either. I cannot get young people to
understand how brief life is, how quickly it passes.

BILLY GRAHAM, CHAPEL SERMON, THE SOUTHERN
BAPTIST THEOLOGICAL SEMINARY, 1982

[13] Come now, you who say, "Today or tomorrow we will go into such and such a town and spend a year there and trade and make a profit"—[14] yet you do not know what tomorrow will bring. What is your life? For you are a mist that appears for a little time and then vanishes. [15] Instead you ought to say, "If the Lord wills, we will live and do this or that." [16] As it is, you boast in your arrogance. All such boasting is evil. [17] So whoever knows the right thing to do and fails to do it, for him it is sin.

JAMES 4:13–17

———

SEVERAL YEARS AGO, I preached through James for the very first time. Few parts of it had as big an impact on me and others as this passage. We considered how older generations of believers often included the phrase "God willing" in their letters or emails. Many used the even more archaic tradition of the Latin form, *D.v.*, which abbreviates *Deo volente*, "God willing." Together, as a church family, we pondered why we are so quick to think we're in charge of our own lives. As we listened to God's word together, we resolved to humble ourselves under God's hand in every area of our lives.

Lesson learned, right?

Soon after that, in March 2020, COVID-19 brought my world crashing down around my ears, as I suspect it did for yours too. After all that time coming to really believe and deeply love the idea of "God willing," why was the loss of my daily routine such a devastating blow? How did the massive alteration of my plans come to be such a crippling shock to the system?

That's what the pandemic was for all of us. Think back to those first weeks as shock and surprise gave way to upset and grief. We began to cross things out of our diaries, and one after another, our best-laid plans for the year and for our lives fell like pins in a bowling alley. Why were we so utterly and completely blindsided?

I think the answer is that as we move through life, the world just constantly dupes us into believing a false story. We become enchanted with a false view of ourselves and the way the world is. Our heads and our Bibles might tell us, "God willing," but we are immersed in the oxygen of the world, which says, "Me willing." I am in charge, and I will decide—and 2020 came like a wrecking ball into our lives to show us just how easily we believed that lie. We presume we are in charge, and so we presume we can plan.

I'm sure you can easily see the root issue here: pride. It is the attitude that says I am the master of my fate, and no one else is. So, from James 4:10 until the end of the letter, James has really only one theme: the content and character of the humble life. He has been showing us the speech of the humble person (4:11–12); now he is going to show us the diary of the humble person (4:13–17); next he will show us the wallet of the humble person (5:1–6); and, finally, the suffering of the humble person (5:7–20).[1]

In this chapter, as we consider James 4:13–17, I will drop two heavy anvils on the oxygen line of the world, which tries unceasingly to keep our pride alive. I hope what you read here plays a part in cutting off that supply line. Instead, James wants us to breathe in the truth of what God says about reality. It is very simple, even stark, but in the simplicity, wholeness is to be found.

I want it to be comforting and life-giving as we see ourselves in God's hands.

Don't Plan Your Life Forgetting What You Are

James begins by simply highlighting our typical diary deliberations, such as "Today or tomorrow we will go into such and such a town" (4:13). These are the daily details and routine decisions we all face: where to go, what to do, when to do it; we have hopes and plans and dreams for every day. James takes us from that canvas of our monthly planners, which we all know so well, and he bursts our bubble with the one big-picture thing we always forget: "Yet you do not know what tomorrow will bring. What is your life? For you are a mist that appears for a little time and then vanishes" (4:14).

I need to ask you, as you sit here reading, have you forgotten what you are? You are a mist, here for "a little time." It's an amazing phrase, isn't it? "A little time"? Three score years and ten, maybe,

God willing. And then you will vanish. We forget this, because we presume we are more than we actually are.

Think back to March 4, 2007. Do you remember the fog that descended on your city that evening?

Neither do I.

Do you recall the dew on the grass that was there on the morning of September 13, 2015? It was fresh and sweet and new, amazing to see. Do you remember it? Surely, you remember that dew, the really special dew?

Of course not.

You probably didn't even notice it. And now it's gone.

Dear reader, James wants you to know what you are. A mist! Here one minute but gone the next. And when you are gone, the world will go on without you.

I saw a picture recently of skyscrapers so tall and magnificent that their top floors were surrounded by mist. It's a good visual image of what we are like, because we live our lives getting these two things the wrong way around: we think we're the skyscrapers; God says we're the mist. We think we're standing tall. We're going to go places, be important, make things, do things. I'm an oak tree; I'm an island; I'm a castle made of granite; I'm a fortress. I want to be master and commander, CEO and partner or company director. The one in charge. The poet William Ernest Henley puts it this way:

> Beyond this place of wrath and tears
> Looms but the Horror of the shade,
> And yet the menace of the years
> Finds and shall find me unafraid.
> It matters not how strait the gate,
> How charged with punishments the scroll,

I am the master of my fate,
I am the captain of my soul.[2]

And what does God say? You're a mist, a vapor.

As for man, his days are like grass;
    he flourishes like a flower of the field;
for the wind passes over it, and it is gone,
    and its place knows it no more. (Ps. 103:15–16)

What was your great-great-grandfather's name? What did he love? What did he hate? What did he do? What did he achieve? Few of us could say. Like the mist, he is gone.

For some of us this is very hard to understand. You're young, and to be young is to feel immortal; you're never going to die. Maybe you're at school or college, or about to get a job or get married, or possibly you have just started a family. The world is your oyster. James says, in fact, that you will float through time and be gone in no time at all.

Others of us are reading this and thinking, "I just blinked, and now here I am in an old person's body!"

James isn't trying to depress us. All he's trying to do is humble us. "Humble yourselves before the Lord, and he will exalt you" (4:10). The brevity of life is one of God's greatest tools for nurturing humility in his creatures.

Do you believe that there are worse things in the world than dying? Worse than dying is living without realizing that I am going to die, not deeply accepting that I will leave this world, and the world will barely remember I was even here.

If this makes us angry or depressed, well, maybe that is our pride rearing its ugly head. Maybe it is the creature rising up to try to be the Creator, trying to be like God, for only the one true and living God is the immortal King. To try to sit on his throne is to get way beyond myself.

While I was writing this book, the pop star Sarah Harding made headline news with her tragic words "I won't see another Christmas." The former Girls Aloud singer had been diagnosed with breast cancer, which spread to other parts of her body. Her diagnosis and treatment were disrupted owing to the pandemic, and she was coming to terms with the brevity of her remaining days. She died on September 5, 2021.

As I recall her story, I wonder what difference it might make to me this year if I believed that I might not live to see next year. If I'm honest, the possibility that I might not do so rarely crosses my mind. I presume that life will continue to stretch ahead of me uninterrupted. James has written these words to wake me up and to remind me that this is no given.

Are you taking the breath in your body for granted? Friend, life is too short to waste on passing trivia. What are you going to do with your life? What of yourself—and of your possessions—are you going to give, gladly, to others? What will be different in God's eternal kingdom this year because of what you choose to do with your time, your money, your resources?

Don't Plan Tomorrow Forgetting Whose You Are

"Instead you ought to say, 'If the Lord wills, we will live and do this or that'" (James 4:15). James is not against planning, of course. It's still part of the life of faith to say that we will do this or that. Planning is good. Fail to plan, then plan to fail, and all of that. But what the Bible is against is how our diaries can make atheists of us all. James is against the kind of self-sufficiency that keeps God for

Sunday but not for Monday to Saturday. It is the kind of planning that means we never stop to think about what difference it will make to my plans to think they might never happen.

Notice the decisive element in verse 15. Observe whom we forget when we plan tomorrow all by ourselves. The Lord. "If the Lord wills . . ."

James is plucking us from our high horses and bringing us down low. He is aiming to drive down deep into my soul the knowledge that I am a character in the story of the world that God is writing, not the author of my own play. God is the author, the playwright, the one painting a glorious picture of all of world history. In the center of this picture is a throne, and there is a King on it, and that King is not you or me. It is the Lord of glory. The point of the world is the Lord Jesus Christ. It is for him and about him, not us.

I wonder if you know this kind of humility. Not the kind that quickly says, "D.v.," or, "God willing," but the kind that says it is because of the Lord's mercies that I am not consumed. My feet touched the ground this morning as I got out of bed, and that was a mercy, and all around me today are more mercies than I can count or ever deserve.

We begin each new year in Trinity Church by saying together questions 1 and 2 of Lord's Day 1 in the Heidelberg Catechism. If you don't know these words, they are worth learning by heart, and I want to shout them from the pulpit every single time we get to say them together:

1. Q. *What is your only comfort in life and death?*

A. That I am not my own, but belong—body and soul, in life and in death—to my faithful Saviour Jesus Christ. He has fully paid for all my sins with his precious blood, and has set me free from the tyranny of the devil. He also watches over me in such a way that not a hair can fall from my head without the will of my Father in heaven: in fact, all things must work together for my salvation. Because I belong to him, Christ, by his Holy Spirit, assures me of eternal life and makes me wholeheartedly willing and ready from now on to live for him.

2. Q. *What must you know to live and die in the joy of this comfort?*

A. Three things: first, how great my sin and misery are; second, how I am set free from all my sins and misery; third, how I am to thank God for such deliverance.[3]

These words have nourished generations of believers down through the centuries, because in the space of a few short lines they fill in the glorious details of the Lord we belong to. His care of us is utterly comprehensive. Every part of us belongs to him. These words are a description of Jesus as Savior, the ultimate rescuer who has freed us from our sins, from the devil, and from fear about what may lie around the corner in the days ahead.

It is the most incredible feeling to be rescued. We recently watched the film *Sully* with our older children. Tom Hanks stars as Captain Chesley "Sully" Sullenberger, the pilot who managed, incredibly, to land US Airways Flight 1549 successfully on the Hudson River after both engines were taken out in a bird strike. Even though we knew how the story ends, the filmmaking was so good that the tension builds and builds, so much so that I could see my sons literally sweating as we watched. I had tears in my eyes as the film's end was interspersed with real-life clips of the drama.

It is the most amazing thing to see people who have come face-to-face with almost-certain death, only to find themselves spared and with their whole lives ahead of them. The film is worth watching for those scenes alone.

I think we so easily forget, as Christians, that this is what life with Jesus is like. We are like the passengers on that plane as it descended toward the Hudson, what most of them presumed would be an icy grave, only to feel the impact and slowly realize they were going to live. Someone had saved them. And someone has saved us. This is our "only comfort in life and death."[4] My comfort does not reside in my own plans or the illusory control I think I have over my life. It comes from belonging to the Lord of glory who laid down his life for my life. Whatever tomorrow holds, he wills, and what he wills, he wills for my good and for his glory.

I am quite sure there are some significant uncertainties in your life right now. Maybe they are casting a long, dark shadow all the way from the future down into the present.

Maybe it has to do with your job, and how impossible it seems to be to find one, or hold on to one, or be happy in one. You belong to the Lord Jesus, and he is watching over you.

Maybe a relationship is just beginning and you are full of optimism and joy, but anxiety is lurking there too. Maybe a very precious relationship has just ended, and facing tomorrow alone feels unbearably bleak. Not a hair of your head can fall to the ground without the will of your Father in heaven, because Jesus is watching over you. He is the good Lord, the tender Master, the gentle Savior, the one who loves you and knows you, and knows what is best and right for you.

Whatever uncertainties you're facing, one healthy spiritual discipline is to check your own internal gratitude meter. We all have one. It is our primary emotional control: Am I grumpy or grateful? One of the things that happens when we deeply, truly, fully, joyfully know whose we are is that gratitude grows and boasting dies.

We come to realize that all of life is a gift we don't deserve, and we just wonder at the mercy and patience and kindness of God.

Questions for Discussion or Personal Reflection

1. Which aspects of your life are you likely to think you have control over?

2. Do you believe there are worse things than dying? Why, or why not?

3. What difference could knowing the brevity of life make to you today? Be as specific as possible.

4. When does planning ahead turn into boasting in arrogance (4:16)? How can you not cross that line?

5. How does knowing you belong to the Lord Jesus change (a) the way you consider the future and (b) the settings of your "own internal gratitude meter"?

8

Wealth

He has all things who has him that has all things.
ANONYMOUS

¹ Come now, you rich, weep and howl for the miseries that are coming upon you. ² Your riches have rotted and your garments are moth-eaten. ³ Your gold and silver have corroded, and their corrosion will be evidence against you and will eat your flesh like fire. You have laid up treasure in the last days. ⁴ Behold, the wages of the laborers who mowed your fields, which you kept back by fraud, are crying out against you, and the cries of the harvesters have reached the ears of the Lord of hosts. ⁵ You have lived on the earth in luxury and in self-indulgence. You have fattened your hearts in a day of slaughter. ⁶ You have condemned and murdered the righteous person. He does not resist you.

JAMES 5:1–6

WORDS CAN PIERCE, heal, endure, snare, satisfy, rebuke, harm, wound, hit, shoot, and more—but words aren't the only tools in the kit.

In this part of James, we're moving from our tongues and our calendars to our money. And money can do so much, as this passage demonstrates. Wealth doesn't just sit there silently. It speaks.

The book of Proverbs tells us that money can deceive, dwindle, grow, and fly. It can be stolen; it can also steal life away. Money can protect, and poverty can pounce. Wages can bring life, and income can bring punishment. Money does so much more than we often realize. It can set us free or make us slaves. Money can discredit a gospel minister and derail a Christian ministry. Money can be what God uses to bring someone to Christ, and it can be what keeps someone out of his kingdom forever.

James is going to show us that money can be what puffs people up with so much pride that they cannot hear and see the things that matter most. Here, again, is how not to be humble: save your money foolishly. Pride in the heart leads to a great big bulge in the wallet.

It is true that great humility and great wealth can coexist. I have witnessed this personally, and it is very beautiful to see these two things living side by side. But I think you will agree that it is also very rare. And it is always a profound shock to the system when we come across people we would expect to be living lavishly who actually live simply.

Many years ago, I shared a house in London with a pastor who had moved his family from Canada while he undertook further ministry training. At the end of his time there he arranged a visit to see John Stott, the well-known and hugely influential Bible teacher and rector emeritus of All Soul's, Langham Place. I don't remember much about my friend's account of his visit, other than his utter astonishment about the scaled-down simplicity of where Stott lived. It made a profound impression on him. He simply couldn't believe that someone so famous, in Christian terms, lived in accommodations quite so meager. They say never meet your heroes, but there is something compellingly attractive about meeting someone like that and realizing there is even more to his grasp of the gospel than is visible from his teaching and writing ministries.

What we do with money—and don't do—preaches visible sermons to the world around us.

Money Talks, but Some Rich People Can't Hear What It's Saying

It's important to notice why I've said "some" rich people. Some. Not all. I don't believe that at this point James has his church in his sights. All the way through he has been careful to make it clear whom he is addressing. In 4:11, once again he was addressing his "brothers," but in 5:1 he simply says, "Come now, you rich." It is a marked and significant change from the family language he has been using so far.

When James is addressing his brothers and sisters, even if they're getting it badly wrong, he keeps calling them to repentance and change, and to stop what they're doing and come back to God: "Draw near to God, and he will draw near to you" (4:8). But here James is simply telling the rich what will happen to them, and I believe he is talking about some rich people, not all. The unrighteous rich. The unbelieving rich. The kind of rich person who deliberately oppresses employees (5:4), takes advantage of them, eats up their pensions as the cream on the top of all his own wealth. It's important to get this right, because James is so forceful and so direct that if

we always assume he is speaking directly to us, we might be plac-
ing ourselves in a firing line he doesn't intend. In God's kindness,
sometimes he wants us to listen in on what he says to others.

I believe that 5:1–6 is just like the words of the Old Testament prophets, where sometimes they denounce the pagan nations
around them, but they deliver the words *to God's people*. Consider
the prophet Isaiah:

> Wail, for the day of the Lord is near;
> as destruction from the Almighty it will come! (13:6)

At this point, Isaiah is actually speaking *about Babylon*, but he says
the words *to Israel*. He wants God's people to know that destruction
is coming for the people who are going to oppress and harm them.

It's an important observation, for it raises the question: Why
address people who aren't even in the room? Why go to all this
trouble to send a deadly arrow through the air if it will not reach
its target? For the rich aren't listening to this: they're on their yachts
in Monaco! "Come now, you rich—can you hear this?—weep and
howl for the miseries that are coming upon you." No, of course
they can't hear, for they're rubbing on the sunscreen! So, why has
James turned up the rhetorical heat?

I think it's because he knows we're sitting in church, but, boy,
we'd love to be in Monaco, wouldn't we? Wouldn't you? I don't
know where you are as you read these lines, but don't be polite
about it. James knows the human heart, skillful soul doctor that
he is. He knows mine, and he knows yours. John Calvin says that
James denounces the rich like this because "he is really looking
to the men of faith, that they may attend to the sad ruin of the
wealthy, and not be envious of their prosperity."[1]

160

There it is: envy. Don't you envy the rich? Bigger house, please. Better school. Best health care. Secure future. Nicer vacations. No overdraft charges. No mortgage. No loan. No more arguments at home over money. No more sleepless nights. No more balancing the books. More reliable car. A few treats. Providing for my children. Don't you envy folks who never have to worry about any of these things?

This passage is here to urge us not to envy the unbelieving, ungodly rich. My dear brothers and sisters, do not envy them.

And here's why: money talks, but some rich people can't hear what it's saying. Read 5:1–6 again, and as you read it, listen to how money is speaking. Twice the text explicitly says that money is talking. First, in verse 3, the corrosion of gold and silver "will be evidence against you." More literally, it will testify against you, cry out against you, bear witness against you. Then, in verse 4, observe how it's the wages "crying out" against the rich. The money in their pockets should be paid out at the end of the day. It is screaming out against the rich: "We're not yours anymore! Pay us! Hand us over to those who have earned us!" Some rich people can't even hear what money is saying.

But what do they think it's saying? We all think money is saying something to us. Consider how wealth is described in these verses: riches, garments, gold, silver. We all believe money is saying to us: "Oh, suits you, sir! You look so good in that . . . you deserve it . . . you are something; you are awesome." Money speaks to us of status, success, achievement, big noise, prestige. We can hear it whispering in our ears by our bonds and our savings, and its murmuring to us with every latest shiny gadget and newest product. Yet, look what James says has already happened to the rich: "Your riches have rotted and your garments are moth-eaten. Your gold and silver have corroded" (5:2–3). The future day of judgment is so certain, so sure, that it's as if the thing in your hand has already turned to dust.

Riches will not last. The rich also die.

By contrast, there are three things that James wants the rich to hear their money saying to them.

First, *don't hoard me.* "You have laid up treasure in the last days" (5:3). You have stored me, stockpiled me in your barns, invested me in IRAs, protected me in insured savings and pension plans. You may have seen the reality TV programs about biggest hoarders. Some houses are just chock full of stuff, paraphernalia in every cupboard. But imagine if it were hundred-dollar bills or gold bullion bars stacked up in each room of your house. Would that be amazing or awful?

Your answer to that question reveals whether you're in tune with what James is saying. The Lord Jesus teaches us to lay up treasures in heaven, not on earth, "for where your treasure is, there your heart will be also" (Matt. 6:19–21). You will not be able to store up earthly treasure and keep your heart whole for God; it will create a split in your affections. James and Jesus speak with the same direct application for our lives. If you want to know where your heart is, then look at where your money is. Is it dispersed to the great good of the gospel in the world, or is it gathering the equivalent of digital dust in an online vault somewhere? For where you locate your money, you will find your heart.

Second, *don't be unjust with me.* "Behold, the wages of the laborers who mowed your fields, which you kept back by fraud, are crying out against you, and the cries of the harvesters have reached the ears of the Lord of hosts" (James 5:4). More than anything else, money buys power; it gets you a seat at the table and provides you with influence. You can do things and go places. And without deliberate checks and balances, the access to power will become the love of power, and the love of power can lead to the hatred of others, expressed in oppression of them.

Third, *don't be self-indulgent with me.* "You have lived on the earth in luxury and in self-indulgence" (5:5). Money makes you self-obsessed. When Karl Lagerfeld, the fashion designer for the House of Chanel, died, he left lots of money to his cat Choupette. She now has her own maids, diamond necklaces, and an Instagram account. It would be funny if it weren't terribly tragic, so revealing of a life utterly turned in on itself.

We live in a society of massive accumulation. It's how we position ourselves in society: the more stuff, the more cars and houses and investments in our portfolios, the more pride we have. But here is what James is getting at by saying that these things rot: hoarding is not what money is for. It's not why God gave it to us. I love these words of John Calvin: "God did not appoint gold to go to waste, or clothes to be eaten by moths, but intended them to sustain human life."[2]

The Bible is not against wealth, and it is not against money, but it is against the love of money. I often say to my own church family that if they can get rich, they should go for it, and as they get rich, never forget why God put the money in their hands. It is to "sustain human life." So, get rich and give big. Earn as much as you can, and give away as much as you can, to sustain as much life as you can.

Whose life are you helping? How many lives? What aid are you giving to others? What are you investing in? Someone has said, "We make a living by what we get, but we make a life by what we give."

So, James is speaking to those who aren't listening—rich people—in the presence of people who should be listening—God's people—to say that we must all hear what money is saying. It is always crying out to us: "Spend me, give me, invest me, use me. Do that with me, and live humbly in God's world, and wholeness will grow in your heart."

One of the most powerful depictions of wealth comes from John Wesley, a famous Christian who set a marvelous example in his own personal generosity with money:

> I was in the robe-chamber, adjoining the House of Lords, when the King put on his robes. His brow was much furrowed with age and quite clouded with care. And is this all the world can give even to a king? All the grandeur it can afford? A blanket of ermine round his shoulders, so heavy and cumbersome he can scarcely move under it! A huge heap of borrowed hair, with a few plates of gold and glittering stones upon his head! Alas, what a bauble is human greatness! And even this will not endure.[3]

Judgment Beckons, but Some Rich People Can't Tell the Time

We need to do more than hear what money is saying: we need to see what time the clock is showing. These verses contain a measurement of time. "You have laid up treasure in the last days" (James 5:3). "You have fattened your hearts in a day of slaughter" (5:5).

James is counting time in days, and he means a certain type of days. The rich are ignorant about this measurement, with no idea what time it is: the last days. The rich are living opulently at present, and as they do so, they are preparing for a day of slaughter, fattening themselves for tomorrow's judgment.

The Bible teaches that when the Lord Jesus Christ died, rose again, and ascended to heaven, God started the clock on the countdown to judgment. The sand in the hourglass started to fall. The enthronement of Jesus in heaven means that the last days on earth are already underway. The phrase "the last days" doesn't mean that at some point we're going to enter a small window of time that's really bad, just before the end. Rather, now that Jesus has come to save, all that is left is for him to come again to judge, to do his one work of being Lord over all the earth. He does that work in two stages: he came once to redeem, and he will come again to complete the rescue of his people and to judge the lost. And James says that this includes the unrighteous rich. The oppressing rich. The luxuriously self-indulgent rich, the proud rich.

"Behold, the wages of the laborers who mowed your fields, which you kept back by fraud, are crying out against you, and the cries of the harvesters have reached the ears of the Lord of hosts" (5:4). There is a stunning twist in this verse. The rich who are maltreating their employees can't hear the money in their loaded back pockets crying out against them, but the workers are crying out too. The cries of the money are falling on deaf ears, but the people's cries are not going unheeded. Far from it. Their cries "have reached the ears of the Lord of hosts."

This should chill the blood. In the Bible, "the Lord of hosts" means the God of armies. Sometimes he's the God of an earthly army, but usually the phrase is there to help us picture God as the commander in chief of the greatest military force the world has ever known. He leads a heavenly legion from the front.

Can you feel the power of what James is saying? That woman in your field, she just looks like a worthless piece of dirt to you, working her fingers to the bone to survive and get by, and you couldn't care less about her. But do you know to whom she's speaking? Do you know who's listening to her? The Lord of heaven and earth who hates the rich oppressing the poor, who detests the powerful trampling on the weak, and who rises in anger against the proud destroying the humble. It is a terrifying place for the rich to be.

Sam Allberry tells the story of the turkey farm near where he lived. It is an idyllic space, surrounded by the rolling green hills of English countryside, with as much fresh air and great food as a turkey could want. There is room to roam, to stretch those turkey legs, and they are free-range to their turkey hearts' content. You can walk past the fence in October and they are happy and plump, clucking away. But walk past the place in January and the same fields are empty. The turkeys are gone. They ate and ate and did not know what time it was. In August, it was warm and beautiful; September was amazing. In October, the turkeys enjoyed heaps of food; in November, even more food. But December rolled around and, for the turkeys, utterly oblivious to the time, the end came.[4]

Every prophet in Israel, every Old Testament prophet who once stood on the stage in Israel's story, every single one of them is gone. Their work in the world is done. As they stood there and warned the people and the nations that judgment was coming, most of the time the people did not even look up from their idolatry, and the nations weren't listening. Yet, one day, the thunder of hooves got louder and louder as the Assyrians and then the Babylonians came and swept them all away. What the prophets said would happen did indeed happen.

Some of you are pastors, and you know what I mean when I say that Sundays seem to roll around relentlessly. It feels as if we are never not preparing to preach, sometimes with little letup; we've been doing this month after month, year after year, without end. Sometimes the unending regularity lessens the sense of privilege and proper perspective on our work. I find it helpful to set the constancy of my preaching in the context of the brevity of my life and the sheer speed at which time is passing and slipping through my fingers. I do not, in fact, have much time left as the minister of my church family. It might not feel like it right now, but my ministry will soon be at an end.

One day every pulpit in every land in every church will fall silent. Every Bible will be closed for the very last time, and judgment will come. The time today, as you read these lines, is "judgment-is-beckoning" time. The world cannot see the reversal that's coming. "You have lived on the earth in luxury and in self-indulgence" (5:5). James is hinting to the ungodly rich that this is their day in the sun, but in the days to come it will be different. It reminds me of Abraham's words to the rich man in Jesus's parable: "Child, remember that you in your lifetime received your good things, and Lazarus in like manner bad things; but now he is comforted here, and you are in anguish" (Luke 16:25).

One day the tables will turn. A swap is coming.

But woe to you who are rich, for you have received your consolation.
  Woe to you who are full now, for you shall be hungry.
  Woe to you who laugh now, for you shall mourn and weep.
(Luke 6:24–25)

This is always how it is when we are friends with Jesus. Life in his kingdom is life in reverse.

Blessed are you who are poor, for yours is the kingdom of God.
  Blessed are you who are hungry now, for you shall be satisfied.

Blessed are you who weep now, for you shall laugh. (Luke 6:20–21)

Several years ago, our family stayed for one night in the home of very wealthy friends. Our children gasped when they arrived and saw the size of the house and the beauty of the gardens. My wife and I were refreshed in the presence of good friends, enjoying delicious food, laughter, and brief respite from responsibilities and pressures. Because they were our friends, all that was theirs was ours. We just loved it.

Christ is the King of the universe, the Lord of glory, and he's yours. What's his is yours. And what did Jesus say? One day you will inherit the earth.

Questions for Discussion or Personal Reflection

1. How does your bank balance and your spending reveal your heart?

2. Can you think of ways in which you have listened to money wrongly, used it unjustly, or spent it self-indulgently?

3. What do you usually think of when you hear the term "last days"? How does this chapter help us keep our money and our spending in right perspective?

4. How can you (and your family) develop a worldview that sees and uses money as an aid to human life? What will that actually look like?

5. Give thanks for the people in your life who have surprised you by their godly use of money.

9

Suffering

The human spirit will not even begin to try to surrender self-will as long as all seems to be well with it.

C. S. LEWIS, *THE PROBLEM OF PAIN*

[7] Be patient, therefore, brothers, until the coming of the Lord. See how the farmer waits for the precious fruit of the earth, being patient about it, until it receives the early and the late rains. [8] You also, be patient. Establish your hearts, for the coming of the Lord is at hand. [9] Do not grumble against one another, brothers, so that you may not be judged; behold, the Judge is standing at the door. [10] As an example of suffering and patience, brothers, take the prophets who spoke in the name of the Lord. [11] Behold, we consider those blessed who remained steadfast. You have heard of the steadfastness of Job, and you have seen the purpose of the Lord, how the Lord is compassionate and merciful.

[12] But above all, my brothers, do not swear, either by heaven or by earth or by any other oath, but let your "yes" be yes and your "no" be no, so that you may not fall under condemnation.

[13] Is anyone among you suffering? Let him pray. Is anyone cheerful? Let him sing praise. [14] Is anyone among you sick? Let him call for the elders of the church, and let them pray over

him, anointing him with oil in the name of the Lord. ¹⁵ And the prayer of faith will save the one who is sick, and the Lord will raise him up. And if he has committed sins, he will be forgiven. ¹⁶ Therefore, confess your sins to one another and pray for one another, that you may be healed. The prayer of a righteous person has great power as it is working. ¹⁷ Elijah was a man with a nature like ours, and he prayed fervently that it might not rain, and for three years and six months it did not rain on the earth. ¹⁸ Then he prayed again, and heaven gave rain, and the earth bore its fruit.

¹⁹ My brothers, if anyone among you wanders from the truth and someone brings him back, ²⁰ let him know that whoever brings back a sinner from his wandering will save his soul from death and will cover a multitude of sins.

JAMES 5:7–20

THE PROBLEM OF EVIL, and the suffering it brings into our lives, is one of the greatest challenges for the Christian faith. How can a good God allow a world of such evil? If he's there, and if he's real, why doesn't he fix what's broken?

These questions become particularly acute when they touch the realm of innocent suffering. This seems like entirely pointless suffering. Take the birth of a stillborn baby: What good can ever possibly come of that? Why does God allow such a thing? Parents approaching the day of the birth with joy and hope and expectation, only to have their child torn from their grasp.

What would you say to parents grieving this kind of loss?

Asking where God is in the midst of such sorrow is a fair question. It is not the inquiry of someone with his or her head in the clouds; rather, such questioning emerges from the reality of life's deep valleys and from the hard reality of bitter tears that won't stop flowing.

I think it's also the kind of question that James would like to try to answer. If it were asked at a university mission lunch bar, James would be the first person to step forward to the microphone. He has a response to that kind of question, but it's one he would want to deliver only with an arm around the questioner's shoulder. For James is writing to suffering Christians, hurting believers, people who follow the Lord Jesus with very real pain in their hearts and with heavy burdens on their shoulders as they follow in his footsteps.

Notice the word "therefore" that appears as part of the command with which the verses begin: "Be patient, therefore, brothers, until the coming of the Lord" (5:7). "Therefore" is a staple. It joins these verses to the immediately preceding verses, where James has been lambasting the rich who are oppressing the poor. The righteous poor, underprivileged believers, are being maltreated at the hands of the powerful rich. So, here is James putting his arm around suffering Christians, and he's about to tell us there is a way to handle it, a way to read it, a way to stand up under it and know God's help in it. Here is how to remain "steadfast" and take your place on God's honors roll for those who have suffered well.

In this chapter I will consider 5:7–12 and 5:13–20 as two parts of one argument. These passages are often separated, of course, usually because the issues in 5:13–20 about praying for healing are so tricky and pastorally complex that they tend to stand up and wave at us for special attention. In fact, however, it is easy to see that, from start to finish, both sections are concerned with the problem of suffering, and we miss something by not reading them together.

In 5:7–12, James sees that suffering can tell us something about our posture before the Lord—it can grow us in steadfastness. In 5:13–20 he sees that suffering can tell us something about our relationship with the Lord—it can expose our sinfulness and re-bellion. In both sections, James has his eye on the different ways suffering can be the Lord's healing medicine for the malady of our divided hearts.

So, let's consider these two aspects of wholeness in turn.

Wholeness Can Be Found in a Surprising Stance Adopted by God's People

The light that James 5:7–12 brings to bear on the pain of suffering is both beautiful and unexpected. I don't know the particular shape of your personal suffering, but I am pretty sure it is present in some form. And if it's not present yet, one day it will be. Here's what James essentially says as he puts his arm around your shoulder: "Can we learn to wait together?" That's what he does here. Here is the help you need in order to wait patiently for the answers you want to your questions. "Can you tell the time?" is what James would say to the student at the lunch bar who asks about suffering. "Do you know what time it is?"

My attempt to capture what James is saying can be summed up like this: if you know who Jesus is, and if you can see where he's standing, then that will make you patient, humble, and steadfast in suffering.

One of the hardest things in the world is being told to be patient. Personally, I find it very difficult. There are some things I find it almost impossible to be patient for, and when I am in pain—emotional or physical pain—being told to be patient doesn't really cut the mustard. The COVID-19 crisis created a global backlog of critical care for patients with serious illnesses, and when such folk are told to be patient, it can raise hackles rather than calm them. And the pandemic itself exposed how we find it almost impossible to wait for things to pass.

There are different types of waiting. Here's the best way I've heard this explained. Imagine you're expecting a letter. While you're waiting for it to drop through your door, there's not much you can do. A friend has posted it, the postal service is doing its thing, and you go about your daily business until it gets there. You are waiting, but the waiting is not shaping your living.

But imagine your dishwasher breaks. You call the repair company, and you survive the three days you have to spend on the phone making it to recorded voice option number sixty-two. At last, you have got them booked in for Tuesday between eight in the morning and noon. How do you wait for that? If you're sensible, you'll live differently because of what you're waiting for. You might take a morning off work, clear your schedule, or arrange for someone else to be there. This is urgent, it's serious, and because of who is coming—the White Goods Knight in Shining Armor—you live in the light of it.

In these verses, it is clear that James is speaking about this second kind of waiting: a form of living today that is profoundly shaped by what we know is coming soon.

The greatest problem we have in our suffering is a poor grasp of who it is we are waiting for, and where he is while we're waiting for him. We are weighed down with all sorts of cares and concerns and heartaches; our tears are real, and we are suffering, and so often suffering impatiently. Why, Lord? How is this possible? Why me? Where are you, Lord? So many questions like these stem from our not letting who Jesus is and where he's standing shape our present living.

Who is Jesus? James calls him "the Lord" four times in these verses. It's a simple way of stressing that we are waiting for the one who is in charge of everything; absolutely everything in all the earth is in Jesus's hands.

More than this, who else is he? As well as Lord, he is "the Judge" (5:9). So, we are not just waiting for the one who is in charge of everything; we're waiting for the one who can fix everything.

This is the glorious gospel: God made it, we broke it, and Jesus fixes it. And his fixing of everything comes in two stages. He came first to deal with sin and pay sin's penalty, but until he comes again, we still live with sin's consequences. There is brokenness at every turn—in our homes, in our wombs, in our cities, in our nation, in our world, in our children, in our parents, in our politicians; among the rich who crush the poor, among the strong who destroy the weak; in our minds, with Alzheimer's that is robbing us of our loved ones right in front of our eyes, and in the depression that just won't lift. You will have your own personal and painful experience of life gone wrong this side of Eden. We live with all of this because, while Jesus has come already as Lord, we still await the day of his coming as Judge.

James wants us to see afresh who the Lord Jesus is and where he's standing. He may not be here physically, and your suffering at the hands of the powerful might be very real, but Jesus has not gone AWOL: he is standing at the door. In saying this, James means that the handle is about to turn, and the door of world history is about to swing on its hinges, and we will meet the Judge of all the earth.

I hope you can feel James's arm around your shoulder for your particular pain. If we know who Jesus is and where he's standing, it can make us patient, humble, and steadfast in suffering.

Maybe you've seen people who have met a judge. They've left the courtroom where the judge was, and now, outside before the media, they are weeping tears of joy and relief. Terrible wrong was inflicted on them; they have known the agony of years of injustice. And then, finally, their moment arrived; the door opened and the judge entered the courtroom. He sifted the evidence, weighed it all, and delivered a verdict that was right and true, proportionate and fitting, and oh, the relief! It is a precious thing to behold.

At the same time, we know this is rare, and justice today is often messy. There are terrible miscarriages of justice in our world, and the scales are not always weighted righteously. There are pains in the human heart that none but Jesus can fix.

Remember the time language from the last chapter, and remember what day it is? These are the last days, the days of preparation before the judgment: "the coming of the Lord is at hand" (5:8). "Near," as some translations say. Just next-door. By the door. It is "judgment-is-coming" time.

I believe this is the Bible's main way of helping us to think in good and godly ways about the problem of suffering. We don't know why God has allowed many things, and the Christian answer to the problem is to say that God has not yet given us the answers. We will not get very far by looking backward if we seek to explain why God allowed suffering. Rather, a proper Christian theology of suffering is a forward-looking perspective. There is a righteous Judge on a throne who rules the world, and he will one day right the universe. When he does so, nothing—absolutely nothing—will escape his gaze.

My friend Andy Gemmill says: "We do not learn from suffering what God is doing in suffering. We learn from the Bible what God is doing in suffering." We can't work out what God is teaching us by looking at what is happening to us. Instead, we work out what we're meant to learn by listening to what God tells us, for the suffering of Christ's people is always there to remind us that Christ the King is coming again.

I find this big picture in James's teaching immensely helpful. It is also a lot to wrap our heads around. So, he gives three examples to help us.

The Farmer

"See how the farmer waits for the precious fruit of the earth, being patient about it, until it receives the early and the late rains" (James 5:7). Farming is tough. All that sweat, all that work, all that labor, waiting for the early rain to be able to plant, then waiting for the later rains to see it all grow and flourish and come safely to harvest. The precious fruit of the earth does not just appear out of thin air. No farmer ever survived without patience. He has to wait for something to come, which, when it comes, brings forth fruit. He waits for rain and, with it, life, joy, and fruitfulness. We are waiting for Jesus to come back, and when he comes, justice, joy, and blessing.

The principle here is that God often asks his people to hold their pain patiently because of what else he is doing. This forms a large part of my answer to the question of where God is in the tragedy of a stillborn baby. Part of the Christian worldview is that the Bible teaches us to weep patiently. I don't have to see the point to know that there must be one, and I don't need to have all the answers to know that God must have them. So, I'm waiting, and with humility. "If the Lord wills, we will live and do this or that" (4:15).

Another part of the answer to this particular question is that sometimes God does give us a glimpse of what he might be doing in the midst of someone's pain. I know of a young mom who had to give up her newborn child for adoption. She was simply unable to care for her baby, but in the agony of her deep grief, who did God give her as the adoptive parents? A couple who some years earlier had experienced a stillbirth. In time, that heartbroken couple came to feel that, in all the trauma of their loss, God was laying the foundations of later comfort and help to that young mom. Initial heartache led to a day several years later when a young couple and a young woman, strangers to each other, were able to weep together, and a precious new life was entrusted into the hands of new parents fitted to give a home and a future to the child. So, two people who had patiently carried deep pain were able to comfort a woman entering deep pain. The comfort was just to be with her, in her company, as a balm because of their own sorrow.

I know this example doesn't cover every angle, nor does it address every individual complexity in its unique circumstances. It certainly doesn't answer everything about suffering and evil, of course. But I find it a helpful encouragement to humility. It helps me to have some perspective, at least, in my pain. It shows me that the signs of what God is doing might be many years down the track, but because he is Lord and Judge, he knows what he is doing. He never wastes our pain.

Sometimes our questions are our way of climbing onto the soapbox of our lives because, if we're honest, we'd like to give God a piece of our mind. But maybe as we do so, we're like a film critic watching thirty seconds of a film and then wanting to lecture the director about his faulty understanding of plot, tension, and character development. There's an absurdity to that, as nearly always what is bewildering in a thirty-second excerpt comes to make sense in light of the whole story.

Maybe if we wait, with humility mingled with our tears, and then learn to wait some more, we could then trust that, with Jesus as Judge, there is precious fruit ahead.

Just like a farmer, so we also need to be patient.

The Prophets

"Do not grumble against one another, brothers, so that you may not be judged; behold, the Judge is standing at the door. As an example of suffering and patience, brothers, take the prophets who spoke in the name of the Lord" (James 5:9–10).

It seems that in the church to which James was writing, the suffering, perhaps at the hands of outsiders, was causing problems inside. They were beginning to turn on each other. Never think that a faithful church, standing up for the gospel, won't be threatened with extinction. We know this from everyday life. When you're under pressure at work, who feels it most? Your colleagues? No. Usually, your spouse suffers because of the day you've had, or your kids have to bear the brunt of your frustrations. We vent the pressure from stress around us onto those closest to us. So, James says, don't "grumble against one another, brothers" (5:9). Don't take out your pain on each other.

From whom did the prophets suffer the most? Their own people! It has been said, "One of the greatest tests of faith in God is the behavior of other believers." I think that's right. For some of us, that's very strange to hear; for others, that is exactly our pain: the behavior of other believers. You might not be in a local church that is tearing itself apart, but you've been bitten and damaged by other believers, and you are sore and your wounds are real. You've ended up more bruised and disillusioned at the hands of some of Christ's people than from enemies of the gospel.

I recently sat with a friend who has been gifted by God as a faithful minister in extraordinary ways, the kind of shepherd any church would be fortunate to have, and he said with tears in his eyes, "I'm just waiting for the next church member to come and hurt me." Sometimes God's people bear more wounds from other sheep inside the church than from the wolves outside it.

Here is where we learn that James's arm around the shoulder is loving, but it is tough love. "Do not grumble against one another, brothers." If we are speaking against others, we cannot be waiting for Jesus rightly. Isn't that what he's saying? I don't know about you, but *I* want to be Lord and Judge all the time—*all the time*. I do not want to wait for King Jesus to sort it all out. I'll sort it out. I'll open my mouth. I'll take it into my hands. I do not want to be patient, and when I am like that, I am so unlike Jesus as Judge. For look how he's described: "compassionate and merciful" (5:11). Judge, yes, but compassionate and merciful to people who have wronged him.

What are we like with people who wrong us?

Job

James finishes his round of examples with Job (James 5:11), and with very good reason, too. For who added insult to injury for Job and rubbed salt into his very raw wounds? His friends! His "comforters" almost tormented him into a false admission of sin, and the entire trauma of suffering in Job's life could have been enough to push him to curse God. He didn't, though, and remained steadfast.

So often I want to sort things out with my own mouth, in my own time, in my own way. It's why this passage ends with the matter of speech again in 5:12. Suffering and corrupted speech go together. We say things we don't mean when we are upset and angry; we call down curses on friends who are now becoming foes, and we speak quickly and rashly to and about one another. Hurt people hurt people. Instead, says James, learn to be people of few words and true words: and nothing more.

Perhaps today as you read, the load you are carrying feels almost too much. We often reach points like this. My prayer is that this part of the word of God will dwell in you richly: "Establish your hearts, for the coming of the Lord is at hand" (5:8). I want to say, as clearly as I can, that one of the ways God heals our divided hearts is by establishing them with the judgment to come. In other words, there is a kind of wholeness available to us in this life that comes from deep, mature, humble, and profound acceptance of the fact that perfect wholeness will be possible only in the next life, on the other side of Jesus's coming again as Judge. This is the kind of wholeness that comes from learning to believe that vengeance belongs to the God who will only ever do what is right. There is a healing of my wounds that can come, in time, from knowing that one day the handle of world history will turn, and the door will swing open to reveal Jesus, the Lord and Judge, who has now come to put everything right.

Such sure trust in what is coming tomorrow does not remove my pain today, but it does serve it notice. It enables me to preach to myself that my agonies are not absolute, and they are not lost on the Lord Jesus. He has seen them and noted them, and he is coming.

Such hope can take a divided, restless heart and establish it for resolute, patient waiting.

Wholeness Can Come from a Shocking
Reality among God's People

In James 5:13–20, the focus remains four-square on God's intention to grow us toward perfection in the presence of suffering, but James now takes a surprising turn in his argument.

This passage is so surprising that many of us have wrestled with it over the years, trying to get our heads around it. I believe the church is worth so much to God—we are so precious to him, so valuable to him, our local church family, every fellowship, the worldwide fellowship of believers—that he will go to any lengths to humble our destructive pride. And sometimes that includes sending the suffering of sickness for sin.

Now, I'm going to say that again because it may be totally unexpected, and you may never have heard it before. We are much more used to hearing from the Bible that our illnesses, our sicknesses, are *not* caused by our sin, and, of course, that is a vital strand of biblical truth. And yet, the Bible says that sometimes, in very particular and specific sorts of cases, sickness in a church family can be caused by sin. On occasions, the lengths God goes to in order to humble and restore his wayward, divided people back to the path of wholeness actually include sending such sickness.

Is anyone among you suffering? Let him pray. Is anyone cheerful? Let him sing praise. Is anyone among you sick? Let him call for the elders of the church, and let them pray over him, anointing him with oil in the name of the Lord. And the prayer of faith will save the one who is sick, and the Lord will raise him up. And if he has committed sins, he will be forgiven. Therefore, confess your sins to one another and pray for one another, that you may be healed. (5:13–16)

All pastors will have examples of either being called upon to carry out the actions described in these verses or being proactive in gathering the elders of the church to pray for someone in this way. We tend to be called upon like this at times of terminal illness, or of long-term debilitating sickness, and the desire to pray for someone in such times is completely understandable, a beautiful expression of both pastoral care and living by faith. I don't believe, however, that these verses are a general description of what we should do when congregation members are sick, or even critically ill.[1]

Just notice how high the stakes are. The "prayer of faith will save the one who is sick, and the Lord will raise him up" (5:15). Twice we are told that the results of praying in this way are certain, and that it will lead to the restoration of the one who is unwell. It seems to me that when we apply this passage to the pastoral care of people who are ill, and we do everything the verses ask of us but there is no healing and the sickness continues, we then have to turn a bit of a blind eye to the strength of the promise in verse 15: "the Lord *will* raise him up." That's what the text says.

This is not a small problem. It is actually the sort of thing that can shipwreck the faith of some. They have carried out all these instructions to the letter, and they have not been healed. Is the problem with our praying? With my elders? Did we anoint with oil in a wrong way? This has happened to many folks: Why is there no healing, Lord, for you said there would be? "The prayer of a righteous person has great power as it is working" (5:16). Verses like this, taken in the wrong way, can cause significantly unhealthy introspection as to whether our prayers have not been answered because we are not righteous enough.

I think James means something different.

Interrogate the text a bit more with me. Why call the elders of the church for sickness? Is there something special about elders when people are ill? And why anoint with oil—what does that do? Why not simply pray? After all, we're told explicitly that it's the *prayer* that saves. There are enough unusual things here to make us sit up and take notice and ask if something else is going on instead.

When we consider the exact wording, we notice that James is mixing the normal language of sin and sickness, and using words from those two different worlds in surprising ways. Look at verse 15. James says, "And the prayer of faith will save the one who is sick." We would expect James to say that the prayer of faith will "heal" the one who is sick, but instead he uses the word "save," the kind of word we use in relation to sins. Such a close connection between sickness and sinning is strengthened by the way the verse ends: "And if he has committed sins, he will be forgiven." Verse 16 does this too, but this time in reverse. Read it again and ask what you would expect to appear as the final word of the first sentence. I think we would expect to find the word "forgiven." Confess your sins and pray for one another that you may be "forgiven," but James says, "that you may be healed."

So, I understand James to be dealing here with a very unusual situation where a church family is quarreling and fighting and destroying each other, so much so that God has sent sickness into their midst as a sign of his judgment. What will now restore them to health is confessing their sins to one another and to the church leadership; they need to repent and come back to God humbly. He is breaking their pride. Sickness often does that to a person. I was so strong, so able, so capable. Now I am so weak, so dependent, so childlike.

Sometimes God's care for his church takes this surprising form.

There are two other examples of this in action, in 1 Corinthians 11 and 1 Kings 17–18.

1 Corinthians 11

"That is why many of you are weak and ill, and some have died" (1 Cor. 11:30).

If there was any church in the New Testament in a worse condition than the one James was writing to, it was the church in Corinth. "When you come together it is not for the better but for the worse" (1 Cor. 11:17). In much the same way as those admonished by James, the believers in Corinth were riven with factions, and their ugly self-interest was spilling out in public displays of selfishness as they ate the Lord's Supper together. The apostle Paul says that such behavior "despise[s] the church of God and humiliate[s] those who have nothing" (1 Cor. 11:22). Although the details are unclear, and we cannot know exactly what form it took, Paul is clear that all of this led to the Lord's judgment of them in a form of discipline that brought weakness, sickness, and death into the church family (1 Cor. 11:30–32). This is how seriously God took their sin.

We know how people react when others whom they treasure are violated. Several years ago, Dr. Larry Nassar was found guilty of abusing young female athletes in his care in the USA gymnastics team. It was a horrid and deeply upsetting experience for the girls and their families to have to relive their ordeals as Nassar was tried in court. At the conclusion of the trial, the father of one of the abused girls was able to contain his anger no longer, and lunged at Nassar in the courtroom. It was an example of indignation and jealous love. Every father, I believe, can understand his emotions, even if, from our positions of detached observation, we would want to counsel that father to not take the law into his own hands.

In such human love we see a flawed and pale reflection of perfect divine love. Zechariah the prophet says about God's love for his people that "he who touches you touches the apple of his eye" (2:8). We must not forget how jealously God loves his people, and how zealous he is to protect the honor of his name and his glory in their midst. There is no malice in God's love, and, unlike us, he does not fly into fits of rage. But neither does he stand idly by and watch his own people destroy themselves and his name. It is striking that when Saul, the persecutor of God's people, met the risen Christ on the Damascus Road, the Lord asked him, "Saul, Saul, why are you persecuting *me*?" (Acts 9:4). So closely is Jesus identified with his people that what befalls them befalls him too.

There are many things on the daily news that make us tremble. We witness awful things all the time. But nothing should chill our blood more than seeing Christ's people trampled by the world. Dictators and presidents and tyrants and warlords who butcher Christ's people touch the apple of God's eye. And if that is true, then maybe nothing in all the earth should make our blood run as cold as when Christian people trample one another.

God can discipline his church for flagrant, persistent, high-handed sin, and for biting, body-destroying selfishness.

1 Kings 17–18

The second example is actually given to us by James himself (5:17–18), and it comes from the life of Elijah in 1 Kings 17–18. Here, Elijah confronts Israel's rotten king Ahab and tells him there will be no rain on the land, and in that very same chapter he raises to life a widow's son. Elijah prays and asks God to raise up the dead boy; God answers his prayer and raises him up.

But notice what James does not say in 5:17. He doesn't say, "Elijah was a man with a nature like ours, and he prayed fervently that God might heal a widow's son." After all, that would be the perfect example of the healing from sickness he has just been speaking about. So, why does James cite a different part of this story and say instead, "He prayed fervently that it might not rain" (5:17)?

Here's why: the removal of rain from the earth in 1 Kings was a sign of God's judgment on the people of Israel. They were suffering a drought; they were sick in body. And it was all because of their sin. More than this, recall how Elijah describes the sin of the people: "How long will you go limping between two different opinions?" (1 Kings 18:21). The context of what James is citing here links the people of God in Elijah's day to the people of God to whom James is writing. These are people who belong to God but have a foot in two worlds, a split in their loyalties, a doubleness in their minds. "If the LORD is God, follow him; but if Baal, then follow him" (1 Kings 18:21).

So, here is what I think James is saying. Elijah was a godly leader in Israel, calling God's people back from God's judgment, telling them to turn back to God in repentance; and as he prayed, God heard his prayer. So, the elders of the church are meant to be the godly shepherds calling a church family that is destroying itself to repent and to come back to God and stop devouring each other. That's why the sick person is told to go to the elders; the anointing with oil was what they did to consecrate someone, to set that person apart as holy. This is a picture of someone who has been destroying the apple of God's eye, brought low in sickness, now being restored and healed through forgiveness as this person confesses his or her sins and gets back on the right path of service and fellowship within the church family. It is a most beautiful picture.[2]

Six Applications of This Message for Us Today

A Word to the Sensitive, Sick Sufferer

We need to be very careful. In general, the Bible does not encourage us to make very direct, causal, one-to-one connections between my sickness and my sin. In John's Gospel, Jesus's disciples ask him about a man blind from birth: "Rabbi, who sinned, this man or his parents, that he was born blind?" (9:2). The answer Jesus gives is that neither sinned (9:3). Job is chided by his comforters to admit that he has done wrong and to confess his sins, but he is absolutely right to refuse to draw this automatic causal connection between sin and suffering.

I want to suggest that if you are ill, and your first impulse is to think, "I must have done something wrong," you are probably not the person James is speaking to here. Some of us are sensitive souls, and we will want to attribute our sorrows to our sins far too quickly.

Instead, let me suggest some diagnostic questions for unearthing a bit more of the kind of situation James is envisaging:

- In the heated argument at church, was I the one driving it with malicious gossip and self-centered assertions?
- Have I been acting in a murderous way toward others, and am I full of bitter jealousy and selfish ambition in the life of the church? Have I been behaving disgracefully toward my brothers and sisters?
- Have I been so proud with my words, my plans, and my wealth that other brothers and sisters are cut to the quick, excluded, and going home hungry?

• Am I playing an active role in sowing division within the church family, and am I actively excluding others in ways that are pushing them to the margins of church life because I refuse to view them as significant and worthwhile?

Now, I'm not expressing matters in strong language like this to excuse our lesser sins. I don't mean to suggest that other ways in which we sin are not also serious. But it is important to grasp just how badly the members of this fellowship were behaving in their public display of church-destroying pride.

I came to my current understanding of these verses while a dear saint in our church family was asking me to bring the elders to her bedside to pray for her. At first, I was sure she either would be immensely disappointed when I shared my hesitation about visiting or would lose herself in introspective worry about the connection between her sickness and her sin. In fact, she found this understanding an immense relief, for she had sought the anointing with oil and prayer from other church elderships over the years without healing and had come to the conclusion that the fault lay in her for her own lack of faith. As we talked together about why this passage might be addressing something different—and as I reassured her that she had not been damaging our fellowship in any way—she actually felt the weight of unrealistic expectations lift from her shoulders.

A Word to the Healthy, Inquisitive Onlooker

Again, we need to be very careful. We should not draw connections between other people's sickness and their sin. I believe it is for the sick person to do this.

Notice it is not even for the elders of the church to do this. Look at what James 5:14 does *not* say: "Is anyone among you sick? Let him expect a visit from the elders at the hospital bed where they will draw the curtains and say, 'Now then, what have you been up to?'" No, it's "Let *him* call for the elders," and the reason is that the sick person is the one who knows his own heart and knows what he's been saying and doing in the church.

I have witnessed a church mess so ugly and so brutal that no one on earth would be able to sort it out unless the people in the thick of it were given grace to read their own hearts and repent—that is, unless they were brought low by God in weakness to confess their sins. I have seen the very people who were destroying a church believe that they were saving it, so utterly blind were they to their own selfishness and pride. Unless somehow God brings such people low into a new place of humble dependence on him, then no number of visits by elders or anyone else speaking to them will show them their sin.

Nevertheless . . .

Nevertheless, we must not qualify these verses into a blunt instrument. James shows that if I were to become seriously and suddenly ill, then it would not be wrong at least to ask if I had been in some way destroying the apple of God's eye. That might be a very unusual thing for you to hear. Maybe until this point it would never have crossed your mind at all that there might be a connection between your health and whether God is pulling at your pride. Please hear me right once again: what we are talking about is the kind of pride that is killing the church—self-aggrandizement, cutting others down to size all the time, trampling over the weak, the poor. It is the further marginalizing of the already marginalized—*in the church*, of all places.

It is no bad thing if sometimes circumstances enter our lives that make us pause and ask, "What have I been doing to God's church, to Christ's bride, his body?"

*If You Know You Have Behaved Disgracefully toward
Another Christian, Then James Is Calling You to Repent*

Come back to the Lord Jesus if you know you have played a role
in damaging the church. I think this takes extraordinary grace, but
God can give such grace to the humble. "Draw near to God, and
he will draw near to you. Cleanse your hands, you sinners, and
purify your hearts, you double-minded" (James 4:8).

If you have been active in the sinful spiraling of disharmony that
can overwhelm a local church, then confess your sins to church
leaders. But look too at 5:16: "Confess your sins to one another
and pray for one another." Martin Luther is believed to have said
that we are to confess our sins to "the Reverend One Another."

Repentance is the family currency and should be in our hearts
always and on our lips often.

*If a Brother or Sister Has Behaved Disgracefully toward
You, Are You Willing to Forgive Him or Her?*

Will you hear the confession of a brother's or sister's sin? The key
is remembering your own status before God as a forgiven sinner.
As I mentioned earlier, Miroslav Volf has said that "forgiveness
flounders because . . . I exclude myself from the community of
sinners."[3] Pride spreads its ugly tentacles in so many directions.
We can be so proud. We behave badly and we forgive slowly. Our
bitterness has become so important to us that we hang on to it; we
enjoy living inside it so much that to take it away from us would
mean we would lose something important. But sickness of mind
and body can come from this kind of introspection.

These might be hard words to hear. The Lord's healing medicine
for the malaise of our divided hearts might be a bitter pill to swallow.

Pray for One Another

As we finish, I want us to see the priority given to prayer in this passage. In fact, prayer is a very important theme in the letter of James (see 1:5–8; 3:9–10; 4:2–3; and here in 5:13–18). Prayer *to* God flows from knowledge *of* God, the one, united, whole God who generously gives good gifts (1:5, 17). This means that James sees prayer as the appropriate response of the humble believer who is seeking God with a whole heart. And here at the end of his letter the contrast between the proud and the humble could not be more stark.

Richard Bauckham explains that one of the reasons why we find prayer difficult in the modern world is that our technology makes us think we have taken control of the world. "Rather like affluence, this assumed position of mastery over the world has deluded modern people into trusting their own capacity to achieve all human ends and has promoted a sense of autonomy and self-sufficiency to which prayer is alien."[4] We don't pray because, ultimately, we don't think we need to. We don't need God. We can be the masters of the universe. But speaking to God in prayer is the ultimate recognition that, in many domains, human powers come to an end. To pray is to confess that not all problems have human solutions, and it is to acknowledge gladly that not all human desires can be realized by human means. In prayer, we "increasingly discover— or rediscover—all things, not as what we possess and make, but as what God gives."[5]

James finishes his letter by encouraging in his readers exactly this kind of lowly abasement before God. He has been explaining the role that suffering can play in bringing about such lowliness. God uses it as a tool because he wants to grow brokenhearted, open-handed, sin-conscious, and grace-dependent believers. Such humility is the posture of the wholehearted, and those who are like this can only cry out to God for help.

So, as we finish, I want to encourage you to take time to consider your posture before the Lord and ask for his help to grow in steadfastness.

Take time to consider your relationship with the Lord and with his people and ask for the grace of humility and repentance where it is needed.

Take time to speak to God in prayer.

Questions for Discussion or Personal Reflection

1. "What time is it?" What is James's answer to this question?

2. How does knowing that Jesus will come back soon to judge help you in your suffering?

3. How do you respond to the idea that God may bring sickness to show someone the extreme sinfulness of his or her actions in the church?

4. What are some of the specific changes you can make to how and why you pray, and to what you pray for?

5. As this book comes to an end, what are some of the main lessons you have learned from the letter of James?

Postscript

[19] My brothers, if anyone among you wanders from the truth and someone brings him back, [20] let him know that whoever brings back a sinner from his wandering will save his soul from death and will cover a multitude of sins.

JAMES 5:19–20

———

NOT LONG AGO, I got lost in the Cairngorm Mountains.

This is not particularly difficult for me. I usually get lost in the car park before even venturing up the mountain, but this occasion worried me a little. It was at the top of Lochnagar, my favorite Munro.[1] When you make this peak, you find yourself on an expansive plateau, from which you can normally go in a few different directions depending on whether you want to bag more Munros or simply begin your descent. On this occasion, however, a cold mist enveloped me out of nowhere, and I couldn't see two feet ahead. I couldn't find the path off the mountain. I was stranded in open space with precipitous drops perilously nearby.

I was both lost and trapped.

All sorts of things go through your head at moments like that: Who knows I'm here, and can they raise an alarm? Now, to be clear, I was never really on the verge of a dramatic mountain rescue. At no point did I fear the worst. I was able to study the map and, after a few wrong turns, pick up a thread of a path to move forward, even if, in the end, my descent would best be described as alternative.

But let me bring this close to home. If it were your closest relative up there—your child, your spouse, your parent—and you knew this loved one were lost in the Cairngorms, what would you do?

It's a question of value. If you made it safely down the mountain and you realized you left your thermos at the very top, well, you would have to be a certain sort of weirdo to go back and get it. Nearly everyone would shrug and say, "That's a shame; now time for a hot bath." But when your child is up there, lost, wandering, we don't even need to wonder what you'll do: search and rescue is the order of the day, with every single means available: lights, helicopters, men, women, ropes, dogs. Without hesitation, off you go to find and retrieve.

Here we are at the end of this book and the end of James's epistle, and as we finish, it is so very important not to lose sight of the wood for the trees. James wants to save his readers from death, from a spiritual disease that threatens to destroy churches from the inside out. We have studied this disease up close and personally over several chapters. These believers are split down the middle, double-minded; they love the world Monday to Saturday, and they love God on Sunday. And they are destroying each other with their proud words, ugly factions, and lifeless faith.

But what are these believers worth to James? "My brothers" (5:19). I find that so striking. When all is said and done, they are "my brothers." It is a question of value. He loves them. They are wandering from the truth, and he loves them enough to try to bring them back.

I hope it is evident that in such a challenging passage it is actually our preciousness to God that is on clear display here and, alongside it, the preciousness of our relationships with each other. These verses are asking: What are we worth to God? What am I worth to you? What are you worth to me? For look how James finishes his letter: "My brothers, if anyone among you wanders from the truth and someone brings him back, let him know that whoever brings back a sinner from his wandering will save his soul from death and will cover a multitude of sins" (5:19–20).

I hope, as you read these lines, that you are worth that to other believers in your life, and I hope others are worth that to you too. Would you go to find a sinner (5:20)? Whom in your own life do you love enough to tell them that what they're doing is sinful, if such words need to be said? Would you put them on your shoulders and carry them home? My prayer is that this letter of James, worked out in our lives, will teach us to love one another enough to live like this. Such love is the way to wholeness in each of our lives. For part of our malaise is our conception of ourselves as islands. We are divided in our loves precisely because we are divided from one another in our lives.

Notice again the responsibilities of both the elders and the Christians under their care: elders are to be willing to pray, and every Christian is to be willing to call for them, and they're to be willing to pray for one another. Elders and pastors have the task of shepherding the most precious living organism on earth. It is why elders meet and pray together for their flocks. It's why we have church membership, and urge it on everyone who is part of our church family, so that sheep can really and truly belong and have shepherds who seek them out by name. Each generation in every local church will come and go from the earth, but the church, the bride of Christ, will exist for eternity. The church is so very precious to God. Pray for your elders as they care for their people; and elders, pray for your people as you care for them.

For underneath it all is this question: What is the church worth to God?

Christian, you have the task of being a brother or sister in the most precious living organism on earth. That is your calling, to live out the family identity that God has given you. Search and rescue is your calling when it's needed, every single time, because that's how much we're worth to each other. You cannot wander away from the truth into error and sin without me coming after you, and I shouldn't be able to do so either without you coming to find me.

So, if you want to pursue wholeness in your life, confess your sins when this is needed. Keep short accounts, but grow long fuses. I love a phrase I heard recently: in your church, be that person who is very easy to please and almost impossible to upset. Use gentle words. Speak words of prayer for one another.

James is clear about what will happen as we live like this: such humility will grow maturity in our hearts, and we will be on the path to wholeness. Radical wholeness.

Notes

Introduction: Getting Your Bearings

1. Raymond C. Ortlund Jr, *Whoredom: God's Unfaithful Wife in Biblical Theology*, New Studies in Biblical Theology 2 (Leicester: Apollos, 1996), 23.
2. Martin Luther, "Preface to the New Testament" (1522), cited in Douglas J. Moo, *The Letter of James*, The Pillar New Testament Commentary (Grand Rapids, MI: Eerdmans, 2000), 43.
3. Luther, "Preface to the New Testament," 43.
4. Both cited in Richard Bauckham, *James* (London and New York: Routledge, 1999), 107.
5. Bauckham, *James*, 108.
6. Moo, *The Letter of James*, 24.
7. Moo, *The Letter of James*, 24.
8. Andy Crouch, *The Tech-Wise Family: Everyday Steps for Putting Technology in Its Proper Place* (Grand Rapids, MI: Baker, 2017), 53.
9. Moo, *The Letter of James*, 62–63.
10. A. Craig Troxel, *With All Your Heart: Orienting Your Mind, Desires, and Will toward Christ* (Wheaton, IL: Crossway, 2020), 19.
11. Troxel, *With All Your Heart*, 20.
12. Bauckham, *James*, 206.
13. The remainder of this introduction builds on David Gibson, "Three Symptoms of a Dying Church: How to Diagnose Your Own Local Body," Desiring God, June 2, 2019, www.desiringGod.org.
14. I am indebted to Dr. Andy Gemmill for his metaphors of "symptoms" and "disease" in reading James. His superb teaching on James is available in several places. See, for instance, www.cornhillscotland.org.uk/, accessed January 12, 2022.

Chapter 1: Perfection

1. Richard Bauckham, *James* (London and New York: Routledge, 1999), 73.
2. Bauckham, *James*, 73.
3. Bauckham, *James*, 177.
4. See the excellent discussion of the role the *Shema* of Deut. 6 plays in James 1:4–18 in Luke Leuk Cheung, *The Genre, Composition and Hermeneutics of the Epistle of James* (Eugene, OR: Wipf and Stock, 2003), 184–93. I am grateful to Ben Castaneda for drawing my attention to Cheung's work.
5. Scott Redd, *The Wholeness Imperative: How Christ Unifies Our Desires, Identity and Impact in the World* (Fearn, Ross-shire: Christian Focus, 2018), 20.
6. Douglas J. Moo, *The Letter of James*, The Pillar New Testament Commentary (Grand Rapids, MI: Ecrdmans, 2000), 56.
7. Jonathan T. Pennington, *The Sermon on the Mount and Human Flourishing: A Theological Commentary* (Grand Rapids, MI: Baker, 2017), 80.
8. Pennington, *The Sermon on the Mount*, 78–79.
9. Pennington, *The Sermon on the Mount*, 153–55.
10. C. S. Lewis, *Mere Christianity* (London: Collins, 1955), 172. *Mere Christianity* by C. S. Lewis copyright © C. S. Lewis Pte Ltd 1942, 1943, 1944, 1952. Extract reprinted by permission.
11. R. Kent Hughes, *James: Faith That Works*, Preaching the Word (Wheaton, IL: Crossway, 1991), 20.
12. Moo, *The Letter of James*, 58.
13. Luke Timothy Johnson, *The Letter of James*, The Anchor Yale Bible (New Haven, CT, and London: Yale University Press, 1995), 179–80.
14. Peter H. Davids, *The Epistle of James: A Commentary on the Greek Text* (Grand Rapids, MI: Eerdmans, 1982), 73.
15. Moo, *The Letter of James*, 58–59; Craig L. Blomberg and Mariam J. Kamell, *James*, Zondervan Exegetical Commentary on the New Testament (Grand Rapids, MI: Zondervan Academic, 2008), 62.
16. Moo, *The Letter of James*, 59.
17. Ben Traynor, "Lead Me Not into Temptation" (sermon on James 1:13–18, Trinity Church, Aberdeen, November 4, 2018), trinityaberdeen.org.uk/sermons/lead-me-not-into-temptation/.
18. If the doctrine of divine simplicity is new to you, I would suggest reading Matthew Barrett, *None Greater: The Undomesticated Attributes of God* (Grand Rapids: MI, Baker, 2019), and Mark Jones, *God Is: A Devotional Guide to the Attributes of God* (Wheaton, IL: Crossway, 2017). To dig a little deeper, don't be put off by the grand-sounding volume by Petrus van Mas-

tricht, *Theoretical-Practical Theology: Faith in the Triune God*, vol. 2 (Grand Rapids, MI: Reformation Heritage, 2019). If you ever wondered how high-flying theology could impact your life, then spend some time in here!

19. Scott Swain, "That Your Joy May Be Full: A Theology of Happiness," Desiring God, April 23, 2018, www.desiringgod.org/.
20. Mastricht, *Theoretical-Practical Theology*, 150.
21. Mastricht, *Theoretical-Practical Theology*, 150.
22. Mastricht, *Theoretical-Practical Theology*, 152.

Chapter 2: Doing

1. Richard Bauckham, *James* (London and New York: Routledge, 1999), 167.
2. Luke Leuk Cheung, *The Genre, Composition and Hermeneutics of the Epistle of James* (Eugene, OR: Wipf and Stock, 2003), 190 (italics added).
3. See the lovely treatment of this in Scott Redd, *The Wholeness Imperative: How Christ Unifies Our Desires, Identity and Impact in the World* (Fearn, Ross-shire: Christian Focus, 2018), chap. 2.
4. C. S. Lewis, *Beyond Personality: The Christian Idea of God* (New York: Macmillan, 1947), 33–38.
5. This point is made by Andy Gemmill in his expositions of James. See www.cornhillscotland.org.uk/.
6. Direct messages.
7. "Bibline," 5 Minutes in Church History, May 5, 2021, www.5minutes inchurchhistory.com/bibline.
8. R. C. Sproul, Twitter, June 30, 2016, https://twitter.com/rcsproul/status /748524506692587520.

Chapter 3: Love

1. See, for example, Greg K. Beale, *The Temple and the Church's Mission: A Biblical Theology of the Dwelling Place of God*, New Studies in Biblical Theology 17 (Nottingham: Apollos, 2004).
2. Marilynne Robinson, *Gilead* (New York: Picador, 2004), 56.
3. Richard Bauckham, *James* (London and New York: Routledge, 1999), 182.
4. Timothy Keller, *Generous Justice: How God's Grace Makes Us Just* (London: Hodder & Stoughton, 2010), 6.

Chapter 4: Seeing

1. Robert L. Plummer, "What Does It Mean That We're 'Justified by Works'? (James 2)," Crossway (website), January 15, 2019, www.crossway.org /articles/are-we-justified-by-grace-or-by-works/.

2. Plummer, "What Does It Mean?"
3. Plummer, "What Does It Mean?"
4. C. L. Mitton, cited in Douglas J. Moo, *The Letter of James*, The Pillar New Testament Commentary (Grand Rapids, MI: Eerdmans, 2000), 130.
5. "Not in Me," text and music by Eric Schumacher and David L. Ward © 2012 ThousandTongues.org. (adm. by Thousand Tongues). All rights reserved. Used by permission.
6. Chris Bruno, *Paul vs. James: What We've Been Missing in the Faith and Works Debate* (Chicago: Moody Publishers, 2019), 74 (italics added).
7. R. Kent Hughes, *James: Faith That Works*, Preaching the Word (Wheaton, IL: Crossway, 1991), 98.
8. The story is originally from Bob Teague, *Live and Off-Color: News Biz* (New York: A&W, 1982), 81–82.

Chapter 5: Words

1. A. Craig Troxel, *With All Your Heart: Orienting Your Mind, Desires, and Will toward Christ* (Wheaton, IL: Crossway, 2020), 181.
2. R. Kent Hughes, *James: Faith That Works*, Preaching the Word (Wheaton, IL: Crossway, 1991), 117.
3. "How Many Words Do We Speak in a Day?," Reference (website), March 28, 2020, https://www.reference.com/world-view/many-words-speak -day-68b7ff8bd0b6943e.

Chapter 6: Wisdom

1. Hannah Anderson, *Humble Roots: How Humility Grows and Nourishes Your Soul* (Chicago: Moody Publishers, 2016), 119–20.
2. Ben Traynor, "True Wisdom" (sermon on James 3:13–18, Trinity Church, Aberdeen, January 27, 2019), trinityaberdeen.org.uk/sermons/ true-wisdom/.
3. *The Larger Catechism* (Fearn, Ross-shire: Christian Focus, 2018), 193.
4. Miroslav Volf, Twitter, April 7, 2016, twitter.com/miroslavvolf/status /718025227918295040.
5. This illustration, with very slightly modernized language here, is found in Philip S. Ross, *Anthems for a Dying Lamb: How Six Psalms (113–118) Became a Songbook for the Last Supper and the Age to Come* (Fearn, Ross-shire: Christian Focus, 2017), 133–34. The remarkable ceremony is viewable online: "'Who's There?—A Poor Sinner': Habsburger Funeral Ritual," Catholicism Pure & Simple (blog), July 24, 2011, catholicismpure.wordpress. com/2011/07/24/whos-there-a-poor-sinner-habsburger-funeral-ritual.

Chapter 7: Presumption

1. For a treatment of James 4:10 that recognizes its structural significance in the letter, see the excellent commentary by Daniel M. Doriani, *James*, Reformed Expository Commentary (Phillipsburg, NJ: P&R, 2007), 141–54.
2. William Ernest Henley, "Invictus," in *A Book of Verses* (London: David Nutt, 1888), 56–57.
3. For an excellent introduction to the Heidelberg Catechism, see Kevin DeYoung, *The Good News We Almost Forgot: Rediscovering the Gospel in a 16th Century Catechism* (Chicago: Moody Publishers, 2010).
4. Question 1, Heidelberg Catechism.

Chapter 8: Wealth

1. John Calvin, *A Harmony of the Gospels: Matthew, Mark and Luke; and The Epistles of James and Jude*, Calvin's New Testament Commentaries, ed. D. W. Torrance and T. F. Torrance (Grand Rapids, MI: Eerdmans, 1995), 305.
2. Calvin, *A Harmony of the Gospels*, 306
3. "*Macbeth* and Thunder at Drury Lane," in *The Journal of John Wesley*, entry for December 23, 1755, www.ccel.org.
4. Sam Allberry, *James for You* (n.p.: Good Book Company, 2015), 129–30.

Chapter 9: Suffering

1. Again, here I am particularly indebted to Andy Gemmill's thinking about this tricky passage. See, for instance, Exposition 3 at www.cornhill scotland.org.uk/, accessed January 27, 2022.
2. For a more traditional reading of this passage (which *does* see it as a model for elders praying and anointing with oil in the case of sickness in the congregation), see Daniel M. Doriani, *James*, Reformed Expository Commentary (Phillipsburg, NJ: P&R, 2007). However, Doriani does note that Scripture can draw a connection between sin and sickness, and he cites as evidence Deut. 28:58–63; Prov. 3:28–35; 13:13–23; Ezek. 18:1–29; John 5:14; Acts 12; 1 Cor. 11:30 (198). His careful treatment of this passage is worth considering as an alternative to mine.
3. Miroslav Volf, Twitter, April 7, 2016, twitter.com/miroslavvolf/status /718025227918295040.
4. Richard Bauckham, *James* (London and New York: Routledge, 1999), 207.
5. Bauckham, *James*, 207–8.

Postscript

1. A Munro is any of the 277 mountains in Scotland that are at least three thousand feet high (approximately 914 meters).

General Index

heart, 13
  as operational headquarters of
    humans, 32–33
  as source of doubleness, 34
Heidelberg Catechism, 153–54
Henley, William Ernest, 150–51
hoarding wealth, 162–63
Howell, Josh, 103–4
Hughes, R. Kent, 51, 103, 111, 123
human flourishing
  and law of God, 69–70
  paradox of, 47
  and Sermon on the Mount, 131
human glory, 87
human intelligence, 84
human strength, 84
human wealth, 84
humility, 120, 136, 137, 142
  from brevity of life, 151
  content and character of, 149
  and great wealth, 158
  in suffering, 172, 175, 178
  takes concrete forms in words,
    137
husbands and wives, words spoken
  between, 124

"in" crowd and "out" crowd, 29
input/output self-evaluation, 66

James, epistle of, 13
  diagnosis of, 31–37
  like book of Proverbs, 113, 121
  on justification, 100–103
  on "my brothers," 194–95
  reveals sin in clear terms, 23
  as strawy epistle, 24
  on symptoms of a troubled
    church, 26–30
  on wholeness, 23–24
jealousy, 134

Jesus Christ
  coming as Judge, 174, 180
  as compassionate and merciful, 179
  as Lord of glory, 88–89
  riches of, 34
  showed no partiality, 88–89
  as wholly true human being,
    35–36
  as Word of God, 112
"Jewish Christianity," 24
Job, steadfastness of, 179
Johnson, Luke Timothy, 53
joy, 48–49
judging, as God judges, 90–93
judging the law, 138–39
judgment, 175, 180
Jülicher, Adolf, 24
justification by faith, 24, 100–103

Keller, Tim, 88
knowing, 32–33

Lagerfeld, Karl, 163
last days, 164–65
law of God, 138–39
  as "law of liberty," 69
  as perfect, 69
Lewis, C. S., 49, 72–73, 169
listening and acting, division between, 33–34
"Lord of glory," 88–89
Lord of hosts, 165
Lord's Supper, 184
love, 79–93
  for enemies, 132
  of glory, 81–83, 84, 85–87
  for God, 44–45
  as God loves, 83–90
  of money, 162–64
  for neighbor, 82–83, 91, 140–41
  for the poor, 91

Scripture Index

Also Available from David Gibson

Drawing on wisdom from Ecclesiastes, David Gibson
persuades us that only with a proper perspective on death can
we find satisfaction in life—and see just how great God is.

For more information, visit **crossway.org**.